Intellectual Property Law in the Czech Republic

Intellectual Property Law in the Czech Republic

Aleš Rozehnal

This book was originally published as a monograph in the International Encyclopaedia of Laws/Intellectual Property Law.

Founding Editor: Roger Blanpain
General Editor: Frank Hendrickx
Volume Editor: Hendrik Vanhees

Wolters Kluwer

The Author

Table of Contents

Table of Contents

List of Abbreviations

BCA	Business Corporation Act
Bulletin	Bulletin of the Industrial Property Office
EU	European Union
GDP	Gross Domestic Product
Institute	Central Institute for Supervising and Testing in Agriculture
Office	Industrial Property Office
TV	Television

List of Abbreviations

Preface

Intellectual property law consists of industrial property law (sometimes also known as industrial rights) and copyright law. Copyright is a set of special private rights and bans, and it also partly interferes with public matters (the role of the state in collective rights management).

Copyrights govern the rights of the author to his work, rights related to copyright, which are the performer's rights to his artistic performance, the right of the audio recording producer to the recording, the right of the audiovisual content producer to his recording, the right of the radio or television (TV) broadcaster to their original broadcast, the right of the publisher to a work yet unpublished where the property rights period has expired, the right of the publisher to remuneration in connection with the making of a copy of his work for personal use, the right of the database creator to his created database, the protection of copyrights and rights related to copyright and the collective management of copyrights and rights related to them.

Copyrights are special personality rights the bearer of which is not just any person but only those who have become an author on grounds of the result of his creative intellectual activity. Copyright is divided into exclusive personality rights, that are associated only with the person of the author and that expire with the death of such person, and exclusive property rights, that are the subject of inheritance.

Industrial property is an absolute right to the intangible results of the process of human creativity, exploration and thinking. Thus, the objects of industrial property are intangible assets, consisting of the results of creativity, research or other activities that are sufficiently unique or original. These are intangible movable things. However, the subject matter of industrial property does not include material substrates on which the intangible asset is captured and which permit the intangible asset to be perceived.

For the industrial property objects to be subject to private law, they must be captured on a material substrate. Material substrates are mostly tangible movable items. The rights to these tangible movable items are governed by legal regulations of the property law. Material substrate can be also the electronic recording of an intangible asset. The rights to the material substrate must, therefore, be distinguished from the rights to the intangible asset that is captured on the material substrate.

Intellectual property objects may be the result of the creative activity of individuals or the result of non-creative activities of natural and legal persons (trademarks, designations of origin, geographical indications). Industrial property may be further subdivided according to its object to the rights to the results of technical or aesthetic creative activities, including inventions, utility models, industrial designs, improvement designs and topographies of semiconductor products, know-how or business secrets and to designation rights including trademarks, designations of origin, geographical indications, a business firm or plant varieties.

Objects of intellectual property are not consumed through their usage, they do not lose functionality and usage does not reduce their quality. Industrial property is, in particular, rights that arise as a result of scientific and technical activities.

The need of formal enrolment in a public list for the purposes of their legal protection is typical for objects of industrial property. Industrial rights are mostly based on a registration principle. Industrial rights are mostly registered by the Industrial Property Office. The so-called right of priority arises by filing the registration. The right of priority establishes procedural advantage of the applicant for the object of industrial property before anyone who would later submit an identical or similar object. The right of priority arises only by submitting an application. In addition, however, it may also be applied within the set period under international treaties.

The right of industrial property forms a part of the private law, but it has a number of public law elements that determine its origin, duration and extinction. Industrial property right is therefore not very different from property right. What is specific is only its subject, which is a specific intangible asset, and the way of creation, which is the registration.

The system of protection of industrial rights is intended to ensure that the owners of new intangible assets have secured the results of their creative mental work. The owner of the object of industrial rights enjoys the same protection as the owner of the industrial rights, with the exception of the right of designation of origin and the geographical indications, which may be exercised by anyone who, within the defined territory, produces production with the required characteristics.

General Introduction

§1. General Background

I. Geography

1. The Czech Republic is an inland country, located in Central Europe, on the northern and eastern hemisphere. Czechia borders with four states (*see* map): Germany (810.3 km), Poland (761.8 km), Austria (466.3 km) and Slovakia (251.8 km). The total border length is 2,290.2 km. The country's surface is formed mostly by heights and uplands; 67% of the territory lies at an altitude below 500 m, 32% between 500 and 1,000 m and approximately 1% above 1,000 m.

2. The territory of Czechia lies along the main European divide, which means that majority of the rivers spring from here and carry water abroad, whereas only a small amount of water flows in from the neighbouring countries. The average long-term national annual precipitation, which is the main water source, is 693 mm. Approximately one-third of this amount is taken away by rivers.

3. Czech climate is mild, borderline between oceanic and continental. Due to the predominant western air flow and the position in relation to the Atlantic Ocean, the continental climate nature rises from the west to the east. However, considering the relatively small area of the territory, the differences between the east and the west and between the north and the south are minor. The local weather and climate are affected much more by height segmentation and altitude. The highly noticeable and regular shifts between the four seasons are a characteristic feature of the climate.

4. The average annual air temperature in the Czech Republic usually ranges from 5.5°C to 9°C, lowlands being the warmest and mountain areas the coldest. Forests currently cover about one-third of the Czech territory, i.e., ca. 25,000 km^2. In the past, they were considerably altered by forestry. Therefore, there are hardly any original forests in the territory of Czechia today. The forests consist mainly of artificial spruce monoculture.

II. Cultural Compositions

5. The Czech nation built its identity in an intentional opposite from the Germans. It emphasized the Old Slavonic spirit of democracy compared to German feudalism. At the beginning of the 1700s, the Czechs lost the top class of society – the Czech aristocracy and the affluent and educated middle class, which had to be recreated with the nation's leaders coming almost exclusively from the intellectual groups. The plebeian nature of the nation, however, remained preserved.

6. The plebeity also represents a frequent source of ideas about the democratic character of the Czech nation. The Czech society may be characterized as egalitarian and collectivistic. It is stratified according to economic and educational status; it is divided into urban and rural segments and further diversified according to political affiliation. The culture of a small farmer's settlement or a small town is very different from the culture in Prague or any of the other bigger cities. The culture of manual workers is very different from the culture of farmers or the culture of the university-educated elite. The Czech society strongly separates public and private life.

7. The Czech nation identifies with the state only in a situation where the state pursues and defends Czech national interests. The Czechs are a traditionally cultural nation because culture served, *inter alia*, also as a protection of national interests; it substituted politics and hence also played a political role. The Czechs do not follow military leaders or monarchs as their role models; they highly value the individuals associated with martyrdom who are still provoking strong emotions.

8. If the Czechs do appreciate any monarch, it would be for their erudition and intelligence. Another tradition highly valued by the Czechs, along with the culture, is non-violence. The Czechs consider themselves as a democratic, cultural, educated, talented, skilful and inventive nation; on the other hand, they attribute to themselves some very negative features, such as envy, conformity, cunningness, selfishness, intolerance and laziness. This ever-present dilemma is a popular topic of Czech art and Czech intellectuals.

9. The long-term dominance of foreign nations over the Czech lands helped to develop a certain degree of hypocrisy as a national feature. Therefore, about the same number of citizens condemns tax evasion and about the same number of them perpetrates it, and the number of citizens condemning corruption is again about the same as the number of citizens who take part in corruption in any form. The Czechs very intensely perceive themselves as the centre of Europe which connects Western and Eastern Europe. Nationalism is viewed in a very negative way; however, the xenophobic atmosphere within the society is far from being suppressed. The Czechs are one of the most agnostic nations in the world.

III. Political System

10. The Czech Republic is a sovereign and unitary state based on parliamentary democracy. The Czech Republic is a democratic legal state with liberal state regime and political system based on free competition of political parties and movements. Its supreme law is the Constitution of the Czech Republic together with the Chart of Fundamental Rights and Freedoms. In its current form, the Constitution has been valid since 1 January 1993, i.e., since the date the independent Czech state was established, as a result of the separation of Czechoslovakia.

11. Power is divided into legislative (Czech Parliament), executive (Czech Government and the President of the Republic) and judicial. The Parliament of the Czech Republic is made up of two chambers – the House of Parliament and the Senate. Every citizen who is at least 18 years old is entitled to vote for candidates to the House of Parliament and the Senate. The House of Parliament is made up of 200 members, who are elected once every four years. The election system is based on the principles of proportionate representation. A new Czech Government is established based on the results of these elections.

12. Every citizen of the Czech Republic, who is entitled to vote and is at least 21 years of age, can be elected to the House of Parliament. Members are elected as representatives of individual political parties; after their election the parties create parliamentary clubs in the House of Parliament. The Senate has eighty-one Senators which are elected with a six-year term of office according to the principles of the majority election system. The elections take place every two years, when one-third of the Senators are newly elected. Every citizen of the Czech Republic, who is entitled to vote and is at least 40 years old, can be elected to the Senate.

13. The Senate is conceived as a counterweight to the House of Parliament, as an element establishing conditions for a better quality legislative process and as an element of parliamentary continuity if the House of Parliament is dissolved. The President of the Republic and the Czech Government are representatives of executive power within the country. The Government is the supreme body of executive power. It is responsible to the House of Parliament for its actions. Besides the Government, ministries and other administrative bodies are also part of the executive power.

14. The actions of the Government issue mainly from the policy statement by the Government, with which the head of the Government appears before the House of Parliament. If this policy is approved and its members express their confidence in the Government during a vote, the Government may start to function and execute matters within its jurisdiction. The President of the Republic is the head of state and the supreme commander of the Armed Forces. A President is elected once every five years in the public vote. Judicial power is executed in the name of the Republic by independent courts of law.

15. During the execution of their function, the judges should be independent, and no one may threaten their objectivity. The court system is made up of the Supreme Court, Supreme Administrative Court, Upper, Regional and District Courts. The Constitutional Court, which is made up of fifteen judges, who are appointed for a term of ten years, oversees adherence to the Constitution. The Czech Republic is a member of the European Union (EU) (among the ten new members since May 2004), Organisation for Economic Co-operation and Development, United Nations Educational, Scientific and Cultural Organization, Visegrád Group, North Atlantic Treaty Organization and other major international organizations.

16. The Czech system of law is part of the continental European system and appertains to the German legal culture. The characteristics of the legal system are the following ones: The main fields of law have been codified (civil and criminal codes, codes of criminal, civil and administrative proceedings, etc.). The system of legal sources is hierarchical, forming a pyramidal structure of legal force within the legal hierarchic and forms a pyramid structure of legal power within the system of law.

17. Written law has been acknowledged as the only source of law, at least in theory. Sources of law are normative legal acts; some international treaties and the Constitutional Court's rulings also have a special function. If sorted out by their legal power, the Constitutional law stands first, followed by other laws, governmental decrees, departmental regulations and generally binding public notices issued by municipalities and regional governments.

IV. Population Statistics

18. The Czech Republic is a politically, economically and socially stable state in Central Europe. With its territorial area (78,864 km^2) and density of population (10.3 million), it belongs to the middle-sized European states. The political status and interests of the Czech Republic on the international scene are determined by its geographical, demographic and economic parameters, efficiency of its international and domestic politics and the extent of its involvement in international relations and the international division of labour.

19. Being a state with an open economy (the proportion of export and service segment in the gross domestic product (GDP) is nearly 55%), but without its own resources of a number of basic raw materials, the Czech Republic is very much dependent on international cooperation. The Czech Republic is a landlocked country situated in Central Europe. It shares its western border with Germany (810 km of border length), its northern border with Poland (762 km), its eastern border with Slovakia (252 km) and its southern border with Austria (466 km). The Czech Republic is situated on the territory of three historical countries (Bohemia, Moravia and a part of Silesia) with a total area of 78,867 km^2. In 2012, approximately 10.5 million inhabitants lived in the Czech Republic. The country is divided into fourteen self-governing regions. The capital city is Prague (*Praha*).

20. According to the Human Development Index, the Czech Republic is a state ranking twenty-seventh on the list of countries with the highest living standard in the world, thus outrunning one of the 'old' European countries, the United Kingdom. The Czech Republic has the eighteenth highest GDP per capita in the EU (thirty-eighth highest GDP per capita in the world); however, the GDP per capita achieved in the Czech Republic still represents just 80% of the average within the EU.

21. According to results of the 2011 census, the majority of the inhabitants of the Czech Republic are Czechs (63.7%), followed by Moravians (4.9%), Slovaks (1.4%), Poles (0.4%), Germans (0.2%) and Silesians (0.1%). As the 'nationality' was an optional item, a substantial number of people left this field blank (26.0%). According to some estimates, there are about 250,000 Romani people in the Czech Republic; co-existence with them sometimes cause social tension. There were 436,116 foreigners officially residing in the country in October 2009, according to the Czech Interior Ministry, with the largest groups being Ukrainian (132,481), Slovak (75,210), Vietnamese (61,102), Russian (29,976), Polish (19,790), German (14,156), Moldovan (10,315), Bulgarian (6,346), Mongolian (5,924), American (5,803), Chinese (5,314), British (4,461), Belarusian (4,441), Serbian (4,098), Romanian (4,021), Kazakh (3,896), Austrian (3,114), Italian (2,580), Dutch (2,553), French (2,356), Croatian (2,351), Bosnian (2,240), Armenian (2,021), Uzbek (1,969), Macedonian (1,787) and Japanese (1,581). There were approximately 4,000 Jews in the Czech Republic in 2005. Estimates of Czech fertility rate in 2012 are among the lowest in the world at 1.27 children per woman. Immigration increased the population by almost 1% in 2007. About 77,000 new foreigners settle down in the Czech Republic every year. Vietnamese immigrants began settling in the Czech Republic during the Communist period, when they were invited as guest workers by the Czechoslovak Government. Today, there are an estimated 70,000 Vietnamese in the Czech Republic. In contrast to Ukrainians, Vietnamese come to the Czech Republic to live permanently and try to integrate in the Czech society.

§2. Historical Background

22. Czech history includes the history of today's Czech Republic, as well as the countries that preceded it and the territory it occupies. The history of human settlement dates back to the Lower Palaeolithic. The first humans of the present type came in the Upper Palaeolithic, i.e., 12,000–40,000 years ago. The oldest inhabitants we know were the Celts, followed by the Germanic peoples and the Slavs. They formed the first political units, Samo's Empire (around 630) and Great Moravia (the ninth century).

23. At that time, Christianity made its way to the Czech territory. In the tenth century, a principality started forming around a tribe in central Bohemia, led by the Pemyslid dynasty. Gradually, it extended and stabilized, got its saints (St. Wenceslaus, St. Ludmila and St. Adalbert) and a bishopric (973), with the Prague Castle becoming its centre. Boleslav I, Wenceslaus' brother and successor, added Moravia to the Pemyslid dominion. At the beginning of the eleventh century, the principality became a fief of the Holy Roman Empire.

24. Ottokar I got the title of a hereditary king, which was certified by the Golden Bull of Sicily (1212). By the murder of Wenceslaus III in 1306, the Pemyslid dynasty died out and the rule of the House of Luxembourg started. The successful monarch Charles IV was one of them, founder of Prague University (1348), the first in Central Europe. However, the following periods witnessed religious wars brought along by the start of Hussitism, a reform movement within Czech Christianity. The movement was started by Jan Hus, burnt in 1415 for alleged heresy; other representatives included Jan Žižka and Prokop Holý. Eventually, the Hussite disputes were settled and Bohemia was ruled by George of Podbrady, a moderate Hussite (1458–1471).

25. Several decades after him, kings of the Jagiellonian dynasty ruled, followed by the House of Habsburg from 1526, who ruled until 1918 and incorporated the Czech lands in a huge empire with a centre in Vienna. In 1618, an unsuccessful Bohemian Revolt led by non-Catholics took place, which resulted in re-Catholization and the destructive Thirty Years' War. In the following Baroque period, the Czech lands experienced a cultural boom; however, Czech was slowly becoming a language of the uneducated only.

26. Empress Maria Theresa (1740–1780) started the Enlightenment reforms, continued by her son, Joseph II (1780–1790). However, she was forced to surrender the majority of Silesia and Klodzko to Prussia. At the end of the eighteenth century, the National Revival started, allowing for the formation of the modern Czech nation as a political power and the revival of the Czech language. In the second half of the nineteenth century, quick modernization and industrialization took place in the Czech territory.

27. The Habsburg Monarchy ceased to exist as a result of World War I (1914–1918). From its ruins, among others, the democratic Czechoslovakia was born (declared on 28 October 1918). Tomáš Garrigue Masaryk was the first President. In 1938, Nazi Germany occupied a part of the territory inhabited mostly by Germans, and the following year it also took the rest of the country. The Protectorate of Bohemia and Moravia was a puppet state in the hands of the Nazis.

28. On the background of World War II (1939–1945), enemies of the regime, Jews and Romanis were killed in large numbers. After liberation by the Soviet and the American armies with a contribution of the Czechoslovak Resistance, Czechoslovakia was renewed in 1945; however, democracy lasted less than three years. In February 1948, there was a coup led by the Communists. In 1968 there was an attempt to democratize the regime, dubbed the Prague Spring, which was defeated on 21 August by military intervention of the Communist countries, led by the Soviet Union.

29. In 1989, the Soviet Bloc got into a crisis and by their Velvet Revolution, the Czechoslovaks managed to bring the Communist regime down without violence. However, they did not manage to keep the state united, and as of 1 January 1993, Czechoslovakia was divided, without violence again, to the Czech Republic and the Slovak Republic. Politically, Czechia joined the West and became a member of the EU in 2004.

Part I. Intellectual Property Law

Chapter 1. Copyright and Neighbouring Rights

§1. Sources: Legislation

30. Copyright is regulated by Copyright Act no. 121/2000 Coll., as amended, and Decree of 16 October 2006, that specifies the types of reproduction devices, types of recorders and the amount of lump sums.

§2. Subject Matter of the Protection

31. The subject matter of copyright is a work. We divide works into two basic groups. The first group includes literary and other artistic works. The second group involves scientific works, which represent a unique outcome of author's creative activity and are expressed in any objectively perceptible form, including the electronic form, permanently or temporarily, regardless of their scope, purpose or significance.

32. The requirement that the work be the result of creative work of an author and be objectively perceptible certainly applies also to literary works and to other artistic works. Not every work must have a material carrier – the so-called material substrate, because work is, e.g., also a musical composition or a verbal work, which may not be recorded as a musical notation or on another sheet or on a record. The requirement of perceptiveness does not need to be met for all persons if it is fulfilled at least for a certain group of people (e.g., a group of people speaking a certain language). If a result meets the definition of work, it always means a work and this fact cannot be ruled out upon agreement of contracting parties.

I. Different Categories of Protected Works

33. A work is, in particular:

(a) a verbal work represented by speech or writing;
(b) a musical work;
(c) a drama work;
(d) a work of music and drama;

(e) a choreographic work;
(f) a work of pantomime;
(g) a photographic work;
(h) a work represented by a process similar to a photograph;
(i) an audiovisual work;
(j) a work of visual art (painting, graphics and sculpture);
(k) a work of architecture;
(l) a work of applied art;
(m) a cartographic work;
(n) a computer program (if it is original in a sense that it is the author's own intellectual creation).

II. Works Excluded of Protection

34. A theme of a work as such, daily news or any other data as such, an idea, a process, a principle, a method, a discovery, a scientific theory, a mathematical or a similar formula, a statistical chart or a know-how are not considered a work. A work also cannot be viewed as a so-called broadcast program, which is a certain type of broadcasting that is repeated, has a given content, a graphical representation of the studio or a type of persons involved in it and is based on a unified know-how. At present, trading with formats is widespread and the price of a successful format is worth millions.

35. Since formats are not protected under Czech law, the Czech radio and TV broadcasters are paying the format authors for the formats (which typically originated abroad) on the basis of courtesy and desire to maintain good relationships with the format owners. However, it is possible for the individual components of the format to be the author's work. The protection of ideas, e.g., TV formats, is more likely to be the cause of unfair competition law. Therefore, if the legal protection of a concept or a TV show format is concerned, such a concept must be identifiable and must be in a stage where it has a potential of commercial utilization. Also, it must be provided to a third party under such circumstances where it would be obvious that its further use is not possible without the author's consent.

36. The following is considered work but the protection under copyright law does not apply to it:

(a) an official work, such as a legal regulation, a decision, a public deed, a public register and a collection of deeds deposited therein, as well as an official draft of an official work and other preparatory official documentation, including official translation of such work, Assembly and Senate publications, municipal chronicles, state symbols and a symbol of territorial self-governing unit, and any other works subject to public interest in exclusion from protection;
(b) creations of traditional folk culture, if the author's true name is not generally known and the work is not anonymous or pseudonymous;
(c) a political speech and a speech delivered during an official meeting.

III. Special Categories of Works

A. *Computer Software*

37. Computer software, regardless of the form of the representation thereof, including preparatory conceptual materials, is protected as a literary work. The ideas and principles upon which any element of a computer software may be based, including those serving as the grounds for the connection thereof with another software, are not protected by copyright.

38. The following are not deemed to be an infringement of copyright to a computer software:

(a) if someone copies, translates, processes, modifies or otherwise changes a computer software, if it is necessary for the utilization of the computer software in compliance with the purpose thereof, including correcting errors of the software, unless otherwise agreed;
(b) if someone makes a backup copy of a software, if it is necessary for the use thereof;
(c) if someone himself or via an authorized person examines, studies or tests the functioning of a computer software in order to figure out the ideas and principles upon which any element of the software is based, if such person does so upon downloading or storing the software into computer memory or upon the display, operation or transmission thereof;
(d) if someone copies a code or translates its form during copying of a computer software or translating it or in other form of processing, modification or other change thereof, either by himself or via a person authorized by that person, provided that such copying or translating is necessary as to obtain the information necessary for the functional interconnection of an independently created computer software with other software and provided that such information is otherwise readily available to such persons and the activity is limited only to those parts of the software that are necessary to achieve the functional interconnection.

39. The reproduction of a computer software is also considered as making a copy that is necessary for downloading and storing the software in the computer memory, as well as for its display, operation and transmission. The information obtained by reproducing the code or translating its form during the software reproduction or during the translation thereof, or during other forms of processing, modification or other change, must not be provided to other persons or used for other purposes other than to achieve the functional interconnection of independently created computer software. Furthermore, the information must not be used for the development, manufacturing or business utilization of substantially similar computer software or to other acts jeopardizing or infringing copyright.

B. Databases

40. A database means a set of independent works, data or other elements organized systematically or methodically and available individually by the electronic or other means, regardless of the form of their representation. Special rights to a database belong to an acquirer of the database, provided that it represents, in terms of quality or quantity, a substantial input for the acquisition, verification or presentation of its content, regardless of whether or not the database or the content thereof is subject to copyright or other forms of protection.

41. A database acquirer has the right to obtain or exploit the entire content of the database or its part, substantial in terms of quality or quantity, and the right to grant a licence to another person to exercise the right. The right of the database acquirer is transferrable. The right of the database acquirer, which was made available to the public in any way, is not interfered with by an authorized user who obtains or exploits parts of the database content or a part thereof, which is insubstantial in terms of quality or quantity, for any purpose whatsoever.

42. It must be ensured, however, that the user makes use of the database in a routine and reasonable manner, not systematically or repeatedly, without prejudice to the legitimate interests of the database acquirer, and that the user causes no harm to the author or bearer of the rights associated with copyright protecting the author's works or other subjects of protection contained in the database. The right of the acquirer of a database made available by this acquirer is also not interfered with by an authorized user who obtains or exploits a substantial part of the database content for his own personal use or for scientific or teaching purposes, provided that the user specifies the source to the extent justified by the non-profit objective pursued, and for the purposes of public safety or administrative or judicial proceedings. The special right of the database acquirer is good for fifteen years following the database acquisition. However, if the database is made available during this period, the special right of the database acquirer extinguishes fifteen years after the first such provision of access to the database concerned.

C. Others

43. With regard to copyright, we also distinguish works of employees, collective works, school works, custom-made works and competitive works. The works of employees mean that the employer exercises, on its behalf and at its costs, the author's proprietary rights to a work created by the author in order to fulfil his obligations arising from the employment or service relationship with the employer or from the working relationship between a cooperative and its member. The employer acquires such rights because it enables the creation of work to its employees due to its material background.

44. The employer may assign the right to exercise copyright to a third party with the permission of the author, except for the assignment of copyright in the sale of a business establishment or a part thereof where the author's permission is not required. The author acquires these rights upon death or cessation to exist of the employer who was authorized to exercise the proprietary rights to an employee's work and has no legal successor. If the employer is not exercising the proprietary rights to an employee's work at all or exercises them insufficiently, the author has the right to request that the employer grants him the licence for such work under standard conditions.

45. The author's personal copyrights to an employee's work are not affected. If the employer exercises the proprietary rights to an employee's work, the author's permission for the publication, editing, processing including translation, integration with another work and placing the work into a collective work, is not required. The employer may also publish the employee's work under its name without the author's permission. The author also does not need to grant the employer his permission to complete his unfinished employee's work in the event that, despite the call for additional performance, the author will be in default with the creation of the employee's work, or if the author's obligation to complete such work extinguishes due to death or subsequent impossibility to perform.

46. The author of an employee's work is entitled to claim a reasonable additional remuneration from the employer in the case where the wage or other remuneration paid by the employer to the author becomes manifestly disproportionate to the profit gained by exercising the rights to the employee's work and the significance of such work for achieving such profit.

47. The collective work is a work where more than one author is involved in it and which is created upon the initiative and under the direction of a natural or a legal entity and presented to the public under its name (this is different from co-authoring), while the contributions included in such work are not usable separately, unlike a collected work.

48. A school or a schooling or educational facility has the right to conclude licence agreements to use a school work under standard conditions. If the author of such school work refuses to grant his permission without a relevant reason, such entities may seek the missing declaration of the author's will at court. The author of a school work may use his work or grant its licence to another person unless it is in conflict with the legitimate interests of the school or the schooling or education facility concerned.

49. A school or schooling or an educational facility is entitled to request that the author of a school work makes an appropriate contribution from the gain obtained by the author in connection with the use of the work or granting of the licence to the costs incurred by the facility concerned to create the work.

50. The audiovisual work is a work created by the arrangement of works utilized in an audiovisual manner, either processed or not processed, consisting of a series of recorded associated images evoking a movement impression, which may be accompanied with a sound and are visually perceptible and, if accompanied by a sound, also audible. The work may be processed and included into an audiovisual work only with the permission of the author. The author of an audiovisual work is deemed to be its director.

51. In the event that the author of an audiovisual work grants the producer of an original record of the audiovisual work his written consent with recording it on the original record, the author thereby also grants the producer an exclusive and unlimited licence to make copies for the purpose of their distribution, use of the audiovisual work in the original, dubbed and subtitled version, as well as with the use of the photographs taken in connection with making of the original record, with an option of granting an authorization forming a part of such a licence to a third party either fully or in part. At the same time, it is assumed that the author and the producer have agreed on a standard compensation.

52. If the author of an audiovisual work, except for a work of music, grants the producer of an original record of an audiovisual work his written consent with including the work into an audiovisual work, the author is thereby granting permission to have the work, either unchanged or processed or subject to other modification, included into an audiovisual work, record it for the original record of such audiovisual work, or dub it or supply it with subtitles.

53. At the same time, the author also grants the producer an exclusive and unlimited licence with respect to making copies for the purpose of their distribution, use of the work and use of the photographs taken in connection with the acquisition of the original record, along with the possibility to grant a third party a licence to use the work fully or in part. By granting the permission, the author thereby confirms to have agreed with the producer of the original record of the audiovisual work concerned on a standard remuneration. The author of an audiovisual work may grant his permission with having the work integrated into another audiovisual work or with integrating it into such a work by himself only upon the expiration of a ten-year period following the permission granted to the producer of the original record of the audiovisual work concerned.

§3. Conditions of Protection

I. Formal Requirements

54. Copyright refers to a completed work, its individual development stages and parts, including the title and names of the characters, provided that the outcomes of the author's creative activity are objectively perceptible. Copyright to a work is established at the moment when the work is represented in any objectively perceptible form. Therefore, the work is created informally, and its existence does not need to be reported or registered anywhere. The work created through the creative processing of another work, including the translation thereof into another language, is also subject to copyright. We refer to these works as derivative works. However, processing is not the use of a theme or an idea which is not a work by itself.

55. The key feature is the informal nature of the protection. Unlike industrial rights, copyright is created informally, so there is no need for any formalities or active acts. Copyright is created automatically at the moment of the creation of work by its author. The author does not need to file any application with any authority or pay a fee and does not need to wait for the results of the registration procedure. Unlike the industrial property rights, the establishment of the protection is simpler and cheaper. However, the disadvantage is that in the case of a copyright dispute, there is no clear evidence in the form of registration of the right in any public register and the author must rely on supporting evidence.

II. Substantive Requirements

56. The law considers the author's work to be a literary work, other work of art and scientific work which is a unique outcome of the author's creative activity and is represented in any objectively perceptible form, including the electronic form, permanently or temporarily, regardless of the scope, purpose or significance thereof. The principle of protection of the form is emphasized in the definition, both by the requirement to represent work in any objectively perceptible form and by stressing the fact that work is protected regardless of the quality of its content. Therefore, even a work that is small, short, of poor quality, sloppy, purposeless, unsaleable or insignificant is formally protected in the same way as a work having a significant scope or value.

57. The list of legal conceptual elements of work according to legal theory includes: (1) the requirement for the work be a result of the author's creative activity, (2) the uniqueness of the work as a result of creative activity, (3) the character of the work be objectively perceived as a result of a creative category of art, (4) the representation of the work in any form perceptible by senses.

58. The term 'creative' indirectly implies that it also involves mental activity which may be supplemented with a mechanical activity. There is no legal definition of creative activity; however, it is clear from the etymological interpretation that it does not involve copying, repeating, mechanical routine or non-creative compilation of works already created by someone else. Creative activity also does not consist in inventing a certain course of action or a solution or in discovering what has already objectively existed. Technical literature highlights the non-legal nature of the artistic or scientific work as it is characterized by a manifestation of human spirit. Sometimes, therefore, the work is referred to as a mental fruit which bears the imprint of its creator's personality.

§4. OWNERSHIP

I. The Author (Initial Authorship)

59. The author is a natural entity who created the work. According to Czech law, the author cannot be a legal entity (as opposed to the countries of common law). Persons other than authors, including legal entities, may exercise copyright but they can never be the copyright bearers. The author of a collected work (e.g., magazine, encyclopaedia, anthology, variety show or exhibition) as a whole is a natural entity who has selected or arranged the work in a creative manner.

60. The author of a work is a natural entity whose real name is typically mentioned on/in the work or listed in an index of the subjects of protection maintained by the respective collective administrator. However, not all copyrights are jointly administrated or, as the case may be, not all authors commissioned a joint administrator with collective administration of their copyrights. In such a case, the work is not registered in the index of the subjects of protection. The fact that the author is a person whose name is mentioned on/in work or in the index of the subjects of protection is a rebuttable assumption, which means that it is valid until the contrary is proven. The rebuttable assumption has been established for the sake of greater legal certainty of users of works. If a work is published on request of the author without mentioning his/her name, it is considered anonymous work.

61. If a work is published under a cover (pen) name or under an artistic mark, it is considered a pseudonymous work. Then, the true identity of the author cannot be disclosed without his consent. Until the author of an anonymous or a pseudonymous work declares himself in public as the author of the work, the person who published the work then represents the author in exercising and protection of copyright to the work on behalf of that person and at his costs.

62. The acquisition of the proprietary right or any other substantive right to a thing through which the work is represented (the so-called material substrate of a work) does not constitute an automatic creation of the right to use the work. The owner or other users of the thing through which the work is represented is not obliged to maintain the thing and protect it against destruction.

II. Joint Works/Works Created by Several Persons

63. The copyright to a work created by joint creative activity of two or more authors until the completion of the work as a single work (the co-authors' work) belongs to all co-authors jointly and severally. Therefore, a co-authors' work is created if the individual parts thereof cannot be used separately and, as opposed to a collected work, they are not separate author's works. A co-author is not a person who contributed to the creation of a work only by providing assistance or advice of a technical, administrative or professional nature, or by providing documentation or technical material, or who only initiated the creation of the work. Also, a co-author cannot be deemed to be a person who only processed the factual material to which the author then gave the form of a work, unless the very composition of the factual material is considered work itself.

64. Co-authorship is also not the case for various authors of a musical and a literary component of one work. In this case, it is not co-authorship but a combination of works. The co-authors decide on the treatment of work unanimously. If one individual co-author prevents the treatment of co-authors' work without a serious reason, the other co-authors may claim the missing declaration of that co-author's will at court.

65. Each individual co-author may seek the protection of copyright to co-authors' work against threats or violation. Unless the co-authors agree otherwise, the share of individual co-authors in the joint proceeds from the copyright to the co-authors' work is proportionate to the size of their creative contributions. If the contributions cannot be distinguished, which is rather frequent due to the relativity of understanding of the creative contributions and the absence of any objective measuring criteria, the shares in the joint proceeds are the same.

III. Works Made for Hire

66. A work made for hire is considered work created upon the contract for work. The customer may use the work made for hire only for the purpose stipulated in the contract. The customer is entitled to use the work beyond the scope of such purpose only upon a licence agreement. The author may use the work made for hire and provide the licence to it to somebody else unless it conflicts with the legitimate interests of the customer and unless it is ruled out by the contract. This applies similarly to the competition work, i.e., the work created upon a public bid.

§5. Transfer

I. Assignment of Copyright

67. According to the applicable legal regulations stipulated by the Copyright Act of the Czech Republic, the proprietary copyrights are not assignable.

68. The proprietary copyright cannot be validly assigned in a translative mode but only as a constitutive act (non-genuinely). It is therefore only admissible to assign partial proprietary copyrights through a licence agreement. A constitutive transfer is a mere 'delegating' of the rights to another person without the author losing his proprietary rights. While the translational assignment results in the extinguishment of the absolute rights and obligations to the subject matter of the assignment in one entity and in the derivative acquisition of the same rights and obligations by another entity, the essence of the constitutive (non-genuine) assignment is not the alienation of the rights but the constitution of the *entitlement to use and enjoy.*

69. In the case of the constitutive assignment, the absolute right to the subject matter of the assignment remains preserved for the assignor; however, the assignor is obliged to refrain from the acts that might prevent proper exercising of the entitlement to use and enjoy acquired by another person. In the case of an exclusive constitutive assignment, the acquirer of the entitlement to use and enjoy is also authorized to refrain from the acts to be carried out towards third parties which form a part of his entitlement to use and enjoy.

70. The constitutive assignment also results in the existence of a consolidation principle, which means that the absolute right affected by the constitutive assignment is once again consolidated into its original form when the entitlement to use and enjoy ceased to exist. If the author assigns his proprietary rights to a third person, such a legal act will be null and void due to conflict with the law.

71. In relation to exclusive personal copyrights, the issue of their assignment is ruled out in terms of concept by virtue of their nature. This corresponds to the general private law principle of the non-assignability of personal rights that are beyond the disposition entitlement of their bearer. As far as the features of a personality are concerned, their alienation, as well as the establishment of an exclusive or non-exclusive entitlement, is ruled out.

72. Due to this exception from the general private law principle of contractual freedom, only the author and no one else can be the copyright owner in his life. Licensing is the only form of the copyright assignment permitted by law, and only in the field of proprietary copyrights.

73. In addition, the principle of translative non-assignability of proprietary copyright also causes the prohibition of other dispositions which may result in the alienation of proprietary copyrights or be a consequence thereof. These concerns, in particular, the prohibition of affecting copyrights by the execution of a decision, prohibition of securing a claim by copyright and specifically the impossibility to put copyright (as well as a work) as a security.

74. The prohibition of alienation does not apply to the claims arising from the relativization of absolute proprietary copyrights, be it the claims arisen on the basis of legal acts (i.e., in particular, licence agreements), other legal facts or unlawful acts (i.e., in particular, copyright offences). These claims are also in principle assignable among the living on the basis of both legal acts and other legal facts (in particular upon a court decision or a decision of a public authority).

II. Licences

75. By a licence agreement, the author grants the licensee the right (the licence) to use the work for individual or for all manners of use within a limited or unlimited scope and the acquirer undertakes to provide the author with compensation. The author cannot grant permission to exercise the right to use the work in a manner which is unknown at the time of the licence agreement execution. For this reason, it is ruled out, e.g., to distribute an older movie via the Internet if the author of this audiovisual work or his heirs did not grant their consent with the distribution. The licensee is obliged to make use of the licence. The licence may be provided as an exclusive or a non-exclusive one.

76. As per the exclusive licence, the author must not grant the licence to a third party and is also obliged to refrain from exercising the right to use the work in a manner for which he granted the licence. In the case of a non-exclusive licence, the author is still entitled to exercise the right to use work in a manner for which he granted the licence as well as to grant the licence to any third parties. A licence agreement by which the author grants the licence to a third party while the exclusive licence of a licensee is still in effect for the same manner of use is null and void without the consent of the exclusive licensee.

77. If so agreed in the licence agreement, the licensee may grant the entitlement which forms a part of the licence to a third party in a whole or in part. In this case, we are speaking about the provision of a so-called sublicence. If the compensation or at least a method of the determination thereof has not been agreed on, the agreement is null and void, except when the parties' negotiation regarding the execution of the agreement shows their will to conclude the agreement, including a compensation, despite the fact that the compensation has not been specified. In such a case, the licensee is obliged to provide the author with a compensation at the rate that is customary at the time of the agreement's execution under the contractual terms similar to the content of the agreement for such a type of work, or the parties should agree in the agreement that the licence is being granted for free.

78. If the compensation has been agreed as depending on the proceeds from the use of the licence, the licensee is obliged to allow the author to check the respective billing or other documentation to ascertain the actual amount. If the licensee provides the author with the information defined by the licensee as confidential, the author must not disclose it to any third party or use it for his own purposes contrary to the purpose for which it was provided.

79. Where the compensation is not determined as depending on the proceeds from the use of the licence, and if it is so low that there is a clear disproportion with the profit gained from the use of the licence and the significance of the work for the achievement of such profit, the author has the right to claim a reasonable additional fee. The licence may be limited to individual uses of the work, while the ways of using the work may be limited in scope and, in particular, in quantity, place or time.

80. Unless otherwise stipulated in the agreement or unless otherwise resulting from the purpose, it is assumed that the territorial scope of the licence is limited to the Czech Republic, the time scope is limited to a standard period which is customary for a given type of work and the manner of use but it cannot exceed one year following the provision of the licence and, if the work is to be turned in after the licence award, then one year following the surrender thereof, and the quantity-related scope of the licence is limited to a quantity that is customary for a given type of work and the manners of use.

81. The licensee must not modify or otherwise change the work, its title or the author's designation. This does not apply, however, if it could be reasonably anticipated that such a modification or other change of the work or the title thereof would be permitted by the author, given the circumstances of the use thereof. In such a case, the licensee must not change the work or the title thereof if the author has reserved the permission also for such changes and the licensee is aware of the reservation.

82. If it is reasonable to request the licensee for the purpose of the work reproduction, and if it is customary, the licensee is obliged to provide the author at its costs at least one copy of the author's work from the copies made by the licensee based on the respective licence (a so-called author's copy). If the licensee does not use the exclusive licence or uses it insufficiently, and if the author's legitimate interests are thus seriously prejudiced, the author may withdraw from the agreement.

83. This does not apply in the case where the failure to use or the insufficient use of the licence is caused by the circumstances existing mostly on the part of the author. The author may withdraw from the agreement on the aforesaid grounds only when he invites the licensee to exploit the licence sufficiently within an adequate deadline following the invitation, and the licensee still fails to exploit the licence sufficiently, despite the author's invitation to do so. In the invitation, the author must notify the licensee about the option to withdraw from the agreement as a result of idle expiration of an adequate deadline.

84. No invitation is required if the exploitation of the licence by the licensee is not possible or if the licensee declares that he will not exploit the licence. The author cannot exercise the right to withdraw from the agreement before the expiration of a two-year period following the licence award; if the work is to be turned in after the licence award, then the two-year period runs following the surrender of the work. A three-month period applies to contributions to daily press and a one-year period applies to other periodical press.

85. The agreement is cancelled on the day of the withdrawal delivery to the licensee. If there are grounds for special consideration, the author is obliged to compensate the licensee for damage incurred by him by the withdrawal. Special attention should be paid in particular to the reasons why the licensee has not sufficiently used the licence. If the licence has not been used at all, the author is obliged to return the fee to the licensee that accepted based on the agreement he intends to withdraw from; if the licence has been used only insufficiently, the author is obliged to return the fee decremented by the part which is due to the actual use with regard to the ratio of the exploited scope of use and the scope stipulated by the agreement or by law.

86. If the licensee was obliged to exploit the licence and breached this obligation, the withdrawal from the agreement is without prejudice to the author's title to a fee. If the fee was agreed as based on the proceeds from the use of the work, the author is entitled to a fee equal to the amount he would have received had the licensee exploited the licence before the withdrawal from the agreement.

87. The author may withdraw from the agreement in writing if his unpublished work no longer corresponds with his beliefs and the publication of the work would aggrieve his legitimate personal interests. The agreement is cancelled on the day of delivery of the written letter of withdrawal to the licensee. The author is obliged to compensate the licensee for the damage he incurred due to the withdrawal. If, following the withdrawal from the agreement, the author shows a renewed interest in using the work; he is obliged to offer the licence first to the licensee under the terms and conditions comparable to those originally negotiated.

88. The licence agreement through which the author grants the licence to copy and distribute a verbal work, a work of music and drama or a work of music, a visual work, photographic work or a work represented in a manner similar to photography, and unless it concerns the use of work performed by performing artists, is an author-publisher licence agreement. Unless the contract stipulates otherwise, it is assumed that the licence is being granted as an exclusive contract; however, this does not apply if it concerns copying and distribution of work in a periodic publication.

89. Prior to the publication of work, the author is entitled to make minor creative changes of the work within a reasonable deadline granted by the publisher, provided that the changes do not result in the publisher's excessive costs or cause a change of the nature of the work (a so-called author's proof). Where the licensee fails to allow the author to carry out the author's proof, the author may withdraw from the agreement if this fact could cause the use of the work in a manner reducing the work's value. If the quantity-related scope of the licence is limited to a certain number of copies and the copies had been already sold before the expiration of the licence term, the licence extinguishes, unless the author and the publisher agree on an increase of the number of copies within six months following the day on which the author invites the licensee to make the respective change of the contract.

§6. Scope of Exclusive Rights

I. Moral Rights

90. The personal copyrights include the right of an author:

(a) to make a decision to publish his work;
(b) to assume authorship, including the right to decide whether and how the authorship should be mentioned upon the publication of his work;
(c) for inviolability of his work, in particular the right to grant consent with any change or an interference to his work;
(d) to author's supervision, which means the right to supervise whether or not the work is being used in a manner reducing the value of the work;
(e) to withdraw from the agreement on the grounds of a change of the author's beliefs;
(f) to carry out author's proof.

91. The author cannot surrender the personal right; these rights are not assignable and extinguish upon author's death. No one can assume authorship of the work after the author's death; the work may be used only in a manner not diminishing its value and the author's name must be properly mentioned unless it is an anonymous work. The protection may be claimed by any person who is a close relative of the author, which means direct relatives, a sibling and a spouse, and other persons within a family or in a similar relationship if the harm suffered by one of them would be reasonably perceived by another person as his own harm. These persons enjoy this entitlement even after the extinguishment of the proprietary copyrights. This protection may always be claimed also by a legal entity associating authors or a respective collective administrator.

II. Exploitation Rights

92. The author has the right to exploit his work and grant another person a contractual licence to exercise this right. Another person may exploit the work without such a licence only in the case of a free exploitation and the so-called statutory licences. The author's right does not extinguish by granting the licence to exploit the work; the author is only obliged to tolerate the interference with the right to exploit the work by another person to the extent resulting from the contract. The author has the right to request that the owner of a thing through which the work is expressed makes it available to the author if necessary for the exercise of copyright. This right cannot be exercised in conflict with the legitimate interests of the owner. The owner is not obliged to surrender such a thing to the author; however, he is obliged, on request and at the costs of the author, to take a photograph or another copy of the work and hand it over to the author.

93. The right to exploit work is:

(a) the right to copy the work, which means making temporary or permanent, direct or indirect copies of work, using any means and in any form whatsoever, for the purpose of making the work available by means of the copies (the work is being copied in particular in the form of a printed, photographic, audial, pictorial or audiovisual copy, or by the construction of an architectural work or in the form of a three-dimensional copy or in the electronic form comprising both analogue and digital representation);
(b) the right to distribute the original or a reproduction of work, which means making the work available in a material form by selling or otherwise assigning the ownership right to the original or the reproduction of the work, including offering it for the purpose thereof;
(c) the right to hire an original or a reproduction of work, which means making it available for the purpose of direct or indirect economic or commercial profit by providing the original or the reproduction of the work for temporary personal use (hiring is not a public use of work against consideration);
(d) the right to lend an original or a copy of work, which means making the work available to public facilities not for the purpose of direct or indirect economic or commercial profit by providing the original or the copy for temporary personal use;
(e) the right to display an original or a copy of work, which means making the work available in a material form by allowing the viewing or other perception of the original or the copy of the work, in particular the work of visual art, photographic work, architectural work including urban work, work of applied art or cartographic work;
(f) the right to communicate the work to public, which means making the work available in a non-material form, live or recorded, by wire (e.g., a cable) or by wireless transmission (e.g., via terrestrial radio and TV broadcasting), or in such a way that anybody can access the work on site and at the time of one's choice, in particular by means of a computer or a similar network (e.g., the Internet), particularly:
  (1) the right to operate the work live or on record and the right to transmit the operation of the work;
  (2) the right to broadcast the work by radio or TV;
  (3) the right to broadcast the radio or TV broadcasting of the work;
  (4) the right to operate the radio or TV broadcasting of the work (it must be noted here that the concept of operating the radio or TV broadcasting is different from the concept stipulated by the act providing for the radio and TV broadcasting operations because under the copyright law, providing an access to a work broadcasted on a radio or a TV using a device that has a technical capacity to receive the radio or TV broadcasting is indeed such an operation. The operation is carried out, e.g., also by a person who has a radio or a TV set placed in his restaurant);
(g) the right to remuneration for the resale of an original copy of a work of art (such as original painting, drawing, portrait, collage, tapestry, engraving, lithography or another graphics, sculpture, ceramics, copyright jewellery, photography or copyright reproduction), which means the author's right to a fee stipulated in a

schedule to the Copyright Act, provided that the resale of a work of art is executed by a gallery operator, an auctioneer or a person exercising his enterprise;

(h) the right to remuneration in connection with the reproduction of a work for personal use, which means transferring the work by means of a device to blank record media or by means of a device for making printed copies on paper or a similar material (in this case, the fee is paid by the producer or importer of the devices for making copies of audial or audiovisual records, printed copies or blank media of audial or audiovisual records, shipper or sender of such devices or carriers and the provider of copying services against consideration, if the copies are printed).

94. The author cannot surrender his proprietary rights; they are non-assignable and cannot be affected by the execution of a decision. However, this does not apply to the claims arisen from such proprietary rights. Proprietary rights are subject to inheritance. If the proprietary rights devolve on the state due to inheritance, they are exercised by the State Cultural Fund of the Czech Republic (*Státní fond kultury*) on its behalf; if audiovisual works are concerned, the proprietary rights are exercised by the State Fund of the Czech Republic for the Support and Development of Czech Cinematography (*Státní fond České republiky pro podporu a rozvoj české kinematografie*).

A. *Reproduction Right*

95. Unless this act stipulates otherwise, the exploitation of a work is not deemed to be the exploitation thereof for personal use of a natural entity whose purpose is not to achieve direct or indirect economic or commercial profit. Therefore, copyright is not interfered with by a person who makes a record, a copy or an imitation of work for one's own personal use. A reproduction or an imitation of a work of visual art made for personal use of a natural person must be always clearly marked as such.

96. The exploitation, however, is the use of computer software or an electronic database also for personal use of a natural person or for internal use of a legal entity or a natural entity conducting enterprise, including making reproductions of such works even for one's own use. Similarly, the exploitation includes the use of a reproduction or an imitation of an architectural work by construction even for personal use of a natural entity or for internal use of a legal entity or an enterprising natural entity and making of a record of an audiovisual work while being operated from a record or a transmission thereof for personal use of a natural entity.

97. Copyright is not interfered with by:

(a) a natural entity who, for his personal use;
(b) a legal entity or a natural entity conducting enterprise who, for its/his own internal use;

(c) he who, upon order for personal use of a natural entity;
(d) he who, upon order for internal use of a legal entity or a natural entity conducting enterprise;

makes a printed reproduction of a work on paper or a similar material using photographic technique or another process with similar effects, except where a published musical notation of a musical work or a work of music and drama is concerned.

98. The number of reproductions made is not limited to one copy. The Czech legislation understands the concept of personal use as the exploitation of a work in the user's privacy. The reproduction for personal use means both the case where the original copy is acquired legally and the case where the model is acquired on the basis of conduct in conflict with copyright.

B. Performing Right

99. Communicating a work to the public is understood as making the work available in a non-material form, live or recorded, by wire or wireless transmission. It also means making the work available to the public in such a way that anybody can access it on site and at the time of one's choice, in particular via computer or a similar network.

100. Live performance of work is understood as providing an access to a work performed live by a performing artist, in particular a literary work performed live, a musical work with or without text performed live or a drama, a work of music and drama, a choreographic or a pantomimic work performed live on stage.

101. Transmission of the live performance of a work is understood as making a work performed live available simultaneously by means of a speaker, a screen or a similar device placed outside the venue of the live performance.

102. Performing a work from a record is understood as making the work available by means of an audial or audiovisual record via a device. Transmission of the performance of a work from a record means making the work available simultaneously from a record by means of a speaker, a screen or a similar device placed outside the place of performance from a record.

103. Broadcasting of a work by radio or TV means making the work available by the original broadcaster via radio or TV and any other such access to the work via any other means serving for the distribution of sound or images and sound or their representation via wire or wireless transmission, including the cable distribution or satellite broadcasting.

104. Transmission of radio or TV broadcasting of a work is understood as making the work available by the simultaneous, complete and unaltered transmission of the broadcasting of the work by radio or TV, via wire or wireless transmission, provided that it is carried out by a person other than the broadcaster. Operating radio or TV broadcasting of a work is understood as accessing the work broadcasted by radio or TV by means of a device that has a technical capacity to receive radio or TV broadcasting. Making a work available to patients in the course of provision of medical services at medical facilities is not considered the operation of radio and TV broadcasting.

C. Adaptation Right

105. The author has the right to grant his permission with any changes or other interference with the work; if the right is exercised by another person but the author upon a contractual or statutory licence, the author may also grant the right to exploit the work in a manner not diminishing its value or the right to the so-called author's supervision, respectively. The means ensuring the author's right to inviolability of work include the author's right to the so-called author's proof.

106. The author's most important means of preserving inviolability of his work is the right to grant another person permission to change or otherwise interfere with the work (the protection of the integrity of work). The licensee (i.e., the acquirer of the licence to exercise the right to exploit work) is limited by the fact that the licensee may modify or otherwise alter the author's designation or modify or otherwise change the work or its title only if it has been so agreed with the author. There is an exception under which the licensee may change or otherwise modify a work or its title if it could be fairly expected that the author would permit such a modification or a change given the circumstance of the use thereof. Even in such a case, however, the licensee cannot make changes or modify the work or its title if the author reserved his consent for this and the licensee has been aware of it.

107. If the user entitled to exploit a work upon a contractual licence makes any change of or interferes with the work, it must not be done in a manner diminishing the value of the work; it applies similarly to the exploitation of a work upon a statutory licence when even in such a case the integrity of work cannot be interfered with in a way that would disrupt the routine exercise of copyright and cause unjustifiable harm to the legitimate interests of the author.

108. The author's right to exploit a work in a manner that does not impair its value is part of the author's personal copyright and as such is directed against any interference with the value of literary works, scientific works and other works of art.

109. One of the means of protecting the right to inviolability of work by copyright is the author's right to perform author's supervision. By exercising this right, the author may ensure that the use of his work by a user will not result in a degrading use or an unauthorized change or a modification of his work. The right to perform author's supervision may be exercised only if this is not ruled out by the nature of the work or the exploitation thereof and, at the same time, provided that the exercise of the right may be fairly requested from a legitimate user of the work.

D. Translation Right

110. The subject of protection also comprises translation of a work. This, however, is without prejudice to the rights of the author of the translated work. A new copyright is created for the translator and, therefore, the copyright of both the translator and the author of the work exist simultaneously next to each other. The author's work may be translated only with the consent of the author, with the exception of work which is no longer protected by copyright.

E. Other Rights

1. *Droit de Suite*

111. In the event that the original of a work of art, which was assigned by the author thereof to the ownership of another person, is further sold for a purchase price exceeding EUR 1,500, and if the seller, buyer or broker of the sale is a gallery operator, auctioneer or another person who systematically deals with works of art, the author has the right to a fee for each (repeated) resale of his work. Within the price range up to EUR 50,000, the fee represents 4% of the purchase price; at higher prices this percentage may be reduced down to 0.25%. The total fee must not be higher than EUR 12,500. The seller and the dealer are liable jointly and severally to pay the fee to a respective collective administrator.

112. The original of a work of art is understood as a visual artwork, in particular a portrait, a drawing, a painting, a collage, a sculpture, an engraving, a lithography or other graphics, photographs, tapestry, ceramics, glass and copyright jewellery, provided that they are made by the author himself or they are reproductions that are considered to be the original copies of the artwork concerned. The reproductions that are deemed to be the original copies of an artwork are the reproductions that have been made in a limited quantity by the author himself or under his supervision, and they are numbered, signed or otherwise declared by the author as genuine. The right to a fee does not apply to the works of architectural design represented by a building structure and works of applied art unless they do meet the characteristics of original artwork and manuscripts of composers and writers.

113. The right to a fee does not apply to the first resale if the seller obtained the original of the artwork directly from the author thereof less than three years prior to such resale, and the purchase price of the original artwork at resale does not exceed EUR 10,000.

114. The author and the collective administrator are entitled to receive any information from a dealer that is necessary to ensure the payment of the fee, including the data serving for the identification of the seller, for a three-year period following the date of the sale. The collective administrator may request the data serving for the identification of the seller only in justified cases, namely in cases where the sale has been challenged, the purchase price has been contested or the dealer fails to pay the fee; the collective administrator must also ensure the protection of personal data provided to him.

115. A dealer who is involved in the sale of an original artwork is obliged to report the sale to a respective collective administrator no later than by the end of January of a calendar year following the year of the sale. The notification under the preceding sentence must contain a specification of the original artworks sold and the purchase price thereof. The fee is payable based on the collective administrator's billing within a deadline that must not be shorter than thirty days unless the collective administrator and the dealer have agreed otherwise.

2. Public Lending Right

116. If a library, an archive or another non-profit schooling, educational and cultural facility makes a reproduction of a work for its archival and conservation purposes, it does not interfere with copyright. Similarly, it is allowed to make temporary or accidental reproductions of a work in electronic form, which does not have an independent economic meaning. However, its purpose must be to make it easier to use the work and its making is an integral and necessary part of the technological process of making the work available, including such a reproduction permitting the efficient functioning of a transmission system, and making a copy of a photographic work, which is a portrait of a person who makes the copy, which was ordered against consideration. It is also permitted to make or allow to make a copy of a published work for non-profit purposes for the needs of handicapped persons within the scope justified by their disability.

117. The interference with copyright does not involve lending original copies or reproductions of published works by libraries, archives or other non-profit, schooling, educational and cultural organizations. Even in this case, however, it is necessary to pay the authors a fee collected by the collective administrators of rights. However, this does not apply to computer software and copies of audio or audiovisual records unless the lending purpose is solely for the needs of handicapped persons with respect to their handicap.

3. Others

118. Other copyrights are jointly administered rights. The purpose of the collective administration of rights is the collective exercise and protection of the proprietary copyrights and the proprietary rights associated with copyright and providing the public with access to the subjects of such rights. The collective administration means the representation of a larger number of persons who have proprietary copyright, or the proprietary right associated with copyright, they are entitled to exercise the proprietary rights to a work or have an exclusive licence to exercise the right jointly managed throughout the force of the proprietary rights and at least within the territory of the Czech Republic.

119. The collective administration of rights also includes the right to grant a sublicence in joint favour of authors upon exercising their proprietary rights to published works or works offered for publication, artistic performances and audio and audiovisual records. However, such a sublicence is possible only where other but the collective exercise of the rights is not permitted or is purposeless. The subject matter of the protection is the one which the right holder announces in writing to a respective collective administrator for the purpose of entering the subject matter of the protection into the index of the subjects of protection.

120. The following are the rights subject to the mandatory collective administration, i.e., the rights which the author cannot exercise by himself but only through a collective administrator:

(a) the right to remuneration for the exploitation of an artistic performance recorded on an audio record issued for the commercial purposes in radio and TV broadcasting;
(b) the right to remuneration for the exploitation of an audio record issued for commercial purposes in radio or TV broadcasting;
(c) the right to remuneration for the making of a reproduction for one's personal use on the basis of an audio or an audiovisual record by transferring its content by means of a device to a blank medium of such a record;
(d) the right to remuneration for the making of a reproduction of a work for one's personal use on the basis of a graphic representation by transferring the reproduction by means of a device serving for making printed copies to another material basis, even through a third party;
(e) the right to remuneration for the resale of an original copy of a work of art;
(f) the right to a reasonable remuneration for the rental of an original copy or a copy of a work or a performance of a performing artist recorded on an audio or an audiovisual record;
(g) the right to exploit works, live performances and performances recorded on an audio record via cable transmission, except for those performances the audio record of which was released for the commercial purposes, and also the right to exploit audiovisual records and audio records via cable transmission other but those released for the commercial purposes. This right is, in fact, a specific case of paid legal licence as the collective administrator, by granting this right, also grants a licence to exploit the subject matter of the protection.

121. The right holders are represented by the respective collective administration in order to exercise these rights as well as to claim the release of unjust enrichment gained upon an unauthorized exercise of the collectively managed right. When distributing and effecting payments of the fees or proceeds from released unjust enrichments collected upon the execution of the mandatory collective administration, the respective collective administrator takes into account only such right holders whose rights to the same subjects of the protection, or to the same types of works, he jointly manages upon a contract or those who applied for registration with him.

122. The collective administrator is a person who has obtained a licence to perform collective administration. It may be a legal entity with its registered office in the Czech Republic which associates, directly or indirectly, the right holders it represents in the collective administration. Collective administration is exercised in a systematic manner, on one's own behalf and on one's own responsibility. Collective administration is not deemed to be an enterprise. Collective administration must be carried out by a collective administrator as the main subject matter of the activity. Granting of the licence to exercise collective administration is subject to a decision of the Ministry of Culture, based upon a written application.

123. The collective administrator represents the right holders on its behalf and on its account. By operation of law, a consignment agreement is thus executed between a right holder and a collective administrator. The collective administrator must exercise collective administration for free but he has the right to be reimbursed for efficiently incurred costs. The operator of a live public music product is obliged to notify the respective collective administrator of the production program, stating the names of authors and works to be performed, no later than ten days prior to the performance is held. If the operator fails to make the notification, the fiction applies that only the works of those authors whose rights are managed by the collective administrator will be played during the performance.

124. The collective administrator grants by contracts the entitlement to exercise the right to exploit the subjects of protection determined either individually or in bulk, which includes all subjects of protection to which he collectively exercises the right. If the collective administrator grants a licence to exercise the right to the subjects of protection determined in bulk, and if the user's data about the exploitation of specific subjects of protection are required for the distribution of the collected fees, the collective administrator is entitled to request such data from the user concerned. Such contracts are called collective agreements.

125. The collective administrator is entitled to prohibit the exploitation of the subjects of protection to which a user would be otherwise entitled to by contract concluded with the collective administrator in the event that the user who is in default with payment of the fee to the collective administrator fails to pay the fee even within an additional thirty-day term granted by the collective administrator for that matter. The collective administrator is entitled to grant the user only a non-exclusive and non-transferrable licence to exercise the right to exploit the subjects of protection.

126. There are currently six entities existing in the Czech Republic that are authorized to operate as collective administrators:

- DILIA – a theatre and literary agency authorized to exercise collective administration for the literary works, drama works, works of music and drama, choreographic works, works of pantomime, audiovisual works, works of visual art of the authors of visual components of audiovisual works, such as directors of photography, architects, stage designers and other authors of audiovisual works, authors of the scenic music specifically composed for the exploitation thereof in a drama work, a choreography work and a pantomime work, except for the scenic music exploited from a sound record released for commercial purposes, scientific works including cartographic works, visual artworks and works of directors of dubbing who are the authors of the spoken component of audiovisual works created in another language.
- OSA – an association for the protection of authors' rights to works of music, which exercises the collective administration of copyright to works of music with or without text.
- INTERGRAM – an independent association of performing artists and producers of audio and audiovisual records, which administrates the rights of performing artists (singers, musicians, actors, dancers, etc.) and producers of audio and audiovisual records.
- OOA-S – an organization for the protection of authors – an association of authors of works of visual art, architecture and visual components of audiovisual works, which administrates copyrights of authors of visual artworks and architectural works.
- GESTOR Civic Association – an association for the protection of authors is a collective administrator of the authors' right to remuneration with respect to resale of original copies of visual art works. The GESTOR Civic Association provides the authors with the collective administration of the right to remuneration with respect to a resale of original copies of visual art works. For the purpose hereof, the original copy of an artwork is namely understood as an original painting, drawing, collage, tapestry, engraving, lithography or other graphics, statue, ceramics, copyright jewellery, photography or copyright reproduction, which is customarily considered the original. The right to remuneration of the authors does not apply to works of architecture, works of applied art and manuscripts by writers and composers.
- OAZA – (*Ochranná asociace zvuka – autor, zapsaný spolek*, an association for the protection of sound engineers, authors) an organization associating masters of sound. Where the requirements have been imposed upon works of art, the masters of sound create works of art and, therefore, they have been granted a licence to exercise the collective administration of rights of the persons who have the proprietary copyright to works of the masters of sound.

127. The activity of the collective administrators is supervised by the Ministry of Culture. It is authorized to request the information and documents from collective administrators that are necessary for the performance of the supervision, and determine whether or not their obligations are being breached. If any defects are ascertained, the Ministry may impose the obligation of remedy and specify a reasonable deadline for the fulfilment thereof. If the Ministry ascertains a breach of obligations of a collective administrator, which are established by law, it may impose a fine up to CZK 50,000 upon the breaching collective administrator. The fine may be imposed repeatedly and no later than one year following the date on which the Ministry ascertained (a subjective time) the breach of obligations, but no later than three years following the date of breach (objective time).

§7. Limitations or Exemptions to the Scope of Copyright Protection

128. The limitation of copyright occurs in cases of reproduction of works and the so-called free use and statutory licences. The limitations of copyright are permitted only in special cases and may be exercised in a manner that would interfere with the standard exercise of copyright and which would be unjustifiable to the detriment of the legitimate interests of the author.

129. A reproduction of a work may be distributed only if the distribution is not gainful. The exploitation of work for one's personal use is not considered interference with copyright (except for making a copy of a computer software or an electronic database or a copy or an imitation of a work of architecture by construction or recording an audiovisual work during the operation thereof). Therefore, the author's consent and the payment of the author's fee is not required in the case of making a record, a reproduction or an imitation of work only for one's own personal use.

130. Although the law speaks of a record, a reproduction or an imitation in singular, it may be inferred that it is possible to make more than one record, reproduction or imitation while still meeting the requirement of personal use. In this case, and provided that a visual artwork is concerned, the reproduction or the imitation thereof must be clearly marked as such; otherwise, it could be a counterfeit. Similarly, the author's consent and the payment of the author's fee (either directly or through collective administrators of rights) is not required for a person who distributes or temporarily makes a reproduction of a work to the extent necessary for the presentation of goods to a customer during the sale of an original or copies of works, copying devices or the works' communication to the public, radio or TV sets and computers.

131. Copyright is not being interfered with even by a person who makes a printed copy on paper or other material using a photographic technique or otherwise with similar effects upon order for the customer's personal use, provided that it is not a published score of a work of music and that the person who made the copy pays the fee for making the copy for personal use properly and on time. A reproduction made for personal use must not be used for a different purpose.

132. The Copyright Act stipulates a number of free statutory licences that enable the exploitation of work without the author's consent and without the need to pay a fee to the author. Such statutory licences are:

(a) citations;

(b) catalogue licence;
(c) the use of a work placed in a public space;
(d) official and news licences;
(e) the exploitation of a work in civic and religious ceremonies, school performances and (the use of a school work);
(f) limitation of copyright to a collected work;
(g) the exploitation of work by reproducing it and by distributing the reproductions thereof;
(h) the use of work by lending/hiring of an original or a reproduction thereof;
(i) the use of an original or a reproduction of a visual artwork or a photographic work by exhibiting it.

133. A citation means a justifiable quotation of excerpts from published works of other authors in one's own work, its inclusion into one's own individual scientific, critical or technical work or to a work intended for teaching purposes, in order to clarify its content, the entire minor published works and the use of a published work in a lecture solely for the scientific, teaching or other educational purposes. However, the author's name must be properly mentioned at all times, unless the quoted work is anonymous, or the name of a person under whose name the work has been made public, as well as the title of the work and a source. The law does not specify the extent of permitted citation. If the work would be composed solely of citations, it would not be a free legal licence.

134. The catalogue licence means the inclusion of an exhibited work in a catalogue of an exhibition, an auction, a trade fair or a similar event; however, only when such an event is being held. However, the author's name must always be properly mentioned, unless the quoted work is anonymous, or the name of a person under whose name the work has been made public, as well as the title of the work and a source.

135. Copyright is also not interfered with by anyone who, by drawing, painting or graphics, photographing or filming, records or expresses a work placed on a square, street, park, public roads or other public space. The author's consent is also not required for the copying, distributing and communicating to the public the work recorded or expressed in this way. This does not apply to the copying or distributing of work in the form of a three-dimensional copy.

136. The official and news licences mean the exploitation of a work for an official purpose on the basis of a law, the exploitation of a work in reporting on a current event in which such a work is operated, displayed or otherwise utilized. The news licence is, in particular, the assumption of a work to periodical press or to another mass media. The news licence also means the assumption or translation of a work into articles or programs with temporal meaning regarding the political, economic or religious affairs already published in another mass media (in periodical press, radio and TV broadcasting, press agency and the Internet). The news licence relates only to the news reporting as a form of presentation of brief current information.

137. An interference with copyright is not deemed to be the non-profit exploitation of a work in civic and religious ceremonies (such as weddings, christening, confirmation, graduation or welcoming newborn citizens), in school performances in which only the pupils, students or teachers of a school or a schooling or an educational facility take part. The same applies to non-profit exploitation of a work created by a pupil or a student, a school or schooling or an educational facility for its internal use. In this case we are speaking of the so-called school work.

138. Unless the author ruled out such a form of exploitation upon the transfer of ownership to an original or a copy of his work, the exhibition or free provision for exhibition represents the last case of the so-called free statutory licence.

§8. Duration of Protection

139. The proprietary rights last throughout the author's life and continue to be in force 70 years after his death. If the work was created as the co-authors' work, the proprietary rights' duration commences upon the death of a co-author who is the last one to survive the other co-authors. The proprietary rights to anonymous and pseudonymous works last for 70 years following the legitimate publication of the work. The proprietary rights to a collective work last for 70 years following the publication thereof. Duration of the proprietary rights to audiovisual work is calculated from the death of the last survivor as follows: director; scriptwriter; author of dialogues; and composer of the music especially created for the use in the audiovisual work concerned. A work where the proprietary rights have expired can be freely used by anyone.

§9. Neighbouring Rights

140. The following are the rights that are not copyrights but related to copyrights:

(a) performer's rights to artistic performances;
(b) the right of an audio record producer to the record;
(c) the right of an audiovisual record's producer to the original record;
(d) the right to a radio or TV broadcaster to the original broadcasting;
(e) the publisher's right to a fee in connection with the promotion of a work published by the publisher for one's personal use;
(f) the right of a database acquirer.

141. Artistic performance is deemed to be the performance of an actor, singer, musician, dancer, conductor, choirmaster, director or some other person who is playing, singing, reciting, exhibiting or otherwise performing an artistic work, including the creations of traditional folk culture. Artistic performance is also considered to be the performance of an artist without performing an artistic performance. A performing artist is a natural person who created an artistic performance. When treating the rights to the performances created jointly upon the performance of the same work by several performing artists, such as members of an orchestra, choir, dance ensemble or other artistic bodies, these performing artists are represented on their behalf and at their costs by an artistic leader as a joint representative thereof. The artistic leader is not a joint representative if most members of an artistic body define another person to be their joint representative. A soloist, a conductor and a director of a theatre performance do not have their joint representative; however, they may act as one. The right of a performing artist is divided into the exclusive personal rights and exclusive proprietary rights.

142. The personal rights of a performing artist include the right to decide to publish his artistic performance. The soloist, if performing by himself, and the conductor, choirmaster, stage director and soloist (if performing along with members of an artistic body) have the right to decide whether and how their name should be stated when publishing their performance. Performers as the members of an artistic body are entitled to this right only in relation to a joint name (a joint pseudonym) under which they jointly create their performance. A performing artist has the right to have his artistic performance, when used by another person, not be used in a manner reducing the performance value. The performer's proprietary rights include the right to exploit his artistic performance and grant a contractual entitlement to exercise the right to another person.

143. The right to exploit an artistic performance means the following:

(a) the right to broadcast and other communication of live performance to the public;
(b) the right to record a live performance;
(c) the right to reproduce a recorded performance;
(d) the right to distribute copies of a recorded performance;
(e) the right to hire copies of a recorded performance;
(f) the right to lend/borrow copies of a recorded performance;
(g) the right to communicate a recorded performance to the public.

144. If someone uses an artistic performance recorded on a sound record and released for the commercial purposes (i.e., distributed by sale) in radio or TV broadcasting, such person does not infringe the right of the performing artist who, however, is entitled to claim a fee for the exploitation of the performance concerned. The performing artist may exercise this right only through a respective collective administrator (*see* below). However, the right of a performing artist is interfered with by a person who, prior to the use of the sound record released for the commercial purposes, does not enter into a contract with the respective collective administrator setting out the amount of the fee for such exploitation and a payment method.

145. The right of a performing artist is also interfered with by a person whom the respective collective administrator has forbidden the continued exploitation of a sound record released for the commercial purposes because that person has been in default with payment for such exploitation and fails to pay the fee even within an additional thirty day time granted to him by the collective administrator for the purpose thereof. Unless the collective administrator limits such a ban to a shorter period, the ban remains in effect until the obligation to pay is met or otherwise extinguishes. If the ban is breached, it will not terminate without the consent of the collective administrator before all claims arising from the breach are settled. The proprietary rights of performing artists last for fifty years following the creation of the performance; however, if a recording of the performance is published during this period, the performer's rights extinguish only fifty years after the publication thereof.

146. Audio record means solely a recording of the sounds of a performing artist's performance perceptible by hearing, or other sounds or the representation thereof. Producer of an audio record is a person who, upon his own responsibility, records for the first time the sounds of a performing artist's performance, or other sounds or the representation thereof, or for whom another person does so upon the producer's initiative. The producer of an audio record has the exclusive proprietary right to exploit his audio record and grant a contractual licence to another person to exercise the right.

147. The right to exploit an audio record is:

(a) the right to copy an audio record;
(b) the right to distribute the original or copies of an audio record;
(c) the right to hire the original or copies of an audio record;
(d) the right to lend/borrow the original or copies of an audio record;
(e) the right to broadcast and otherwise communicate an audio record to the public.

The right of an audio record's producer is transferrable and lasts for fifty years following the making of the audio record; however, if the audio record is published during the fifty-year period, the producer's right extinguishes only fifty years after the publication thereof.

148. Audiovisual record is a record of an audiovisual work or a record of another series of recorded associated images making the impression of a movement, accompanied with a sound or without a sound, perceptible by sight and, if accompanied by a sound, also perceptible by hearing. The producer of an audiovisual record is a person who, upon his responsibility, makes an audiovisual record for the first time or for whom another person does so upon the producer's initiative. The producer of an audiovisual record has the exclusive proprietary right to exploit his audiovisual record and grant a contractual licence to another person to exercise the right.

149. The right to exploit an audiovisual record is:

(a) the right to copy an audiovisual record;
(b) the right to distribute the original or copies of an audiovisual record;
(c) the right to hire the original or copies of an audiovisual record;
(d) the right to lend/borrow the original or copies of an audiovisual record;
(e) the right to broadcast and otherwise communicate an audiovisual record to the public.

The right of an audiovisual record's producer is transferrable and lasts for fifty years following the making of the audiovisual recording; however, if the audiovisual record is published during the fifty-year period, the producer's right extinguishes only fifty years after the publication thereof.

150. Broadcasting, in a sense of copyright, is understood as the outcome of the sound, or image and sounds distribution, or their representation via radio or TV for the reception by the public. Therefore, this is a different understanding of broadcasting than that contained in the Radio and Television Broadcasting Act. Here, broadcasting is not understood as an activity but as a certain result of an activity. A broadcaster is a person who, upon his responsibility, performs broadcasting of sounds, or images and sounds, by means of radio or TV, or for whom another person does so upon the broadcaster's initiative. The broadcaster has the exclusive proprietary right to exploit his broadcasting and grant a contractual licence to exercise this right to another person.

151. The right to exploit broadcasting is:

(a) the right to record a broadcasting;
(b) the right to copy a recorded broadcasting;
(c) the right to distribute copies of a recorded broadcasting;
(d) the right to communicate a broadcasting to the public.

The broadcaster's right is transferrable and lasts for fifty years after the first broadcasting is made.

152. The publisher has the right to a fee in connection with making a copy of a work published by him for his personal use. The right is good for fifty years following the publication of the work.

§10. Infringement and Remedies

153. Any interference with the personal or proprietary rights constitutes an infringement of copyright; however, the range of possible copyright interferences is not thereby exhausted. Where a person develops, produces, offers for sale, rent or lease, or imports, distributes or utilizes an equipment intended to remove, put out of operation or restrict the functionality of technical devices or other means (coding apparatus) to achieve property benefit, which are to prevent, restrict or avoid unauthorized interference with copyright to a work that is made accessible only with the use of a code, such person interferes with copyright.

154. An unauthorized interference with copyright is also understood as the removal or change of any electronic information about the identification of rights to a work and the distribution of a copy of work, including the import thereof, as well as the communication of a work to the public, where the electronic information about the identification of rights to a work was removed or changed without the author's consent. An unauthorized interference with copyright also occurs when a person uses a title or an external modification for his work which is already being used legitimately by another author for the same kind of work, if it could cause a threat of likelihood of confusion of both works, unless it results otherwise from the nature or the determination of the work concerned.

155. An author whose rights have been interfered with or whose rights are threatened by an interference therewith may file an action to:

(a) determine his authorship, while the author is not required to prove an urgent legal interest in the determination thereof;
(b) declare the prohibition of endangering his right, including impending repetition or unauthorized interference with his right, in particular the prohibition of unauthorized production, unauthorized commercial sale, unauthorized import or export of an original or a copy or an imitation of a work, unauthorized communication of a work to the public, as well as an unauthorized promotion, including advertisement and other commercials;
(c) disclose the data about the origin of a copy or an imitation of a work made without authorization, about the method and extent of the exploitation thereof and about the identity of the person involved in the unauthorized production or the distribution, respectively;
(d) publish a judgment at the expense of the unsuccessful party, provided that the author succeeded in the matter, and, depending on the circumstances, determine the scope, form and method of publication;
(e) be compensated for damages;
(f) release unjust enrichment equal to a double of the fee that would be customary for obtaining the licence to a work at the time of the unauthorized treatment of work;
(g) replace the declaration of will of a co-author who obstructs the treatment of a work produced by other co-authors without having a serious reason;
(h) remove the consequences of an interference with the right, in particular:
    (1) by withdrawing a copy or an imitation of a work made without authorization, or a tool intended for the removal of the protection of a work from trading or other forms of exploitation;
    (2) by destroying a copy or an imitation of a work made without authorization, or a tool intended for the removal of the protection of a work;
(i) provide a reasonable satisfaction for a non-pecuniary damage, in particular:
    (1) offering an apology;

(2) offering a pecuniary satisfaction, provided that awarding of another form of satisfaction would not appear to be sufficient; the amount of the pecuniary satisfaction is determined by court which shall also take into account the seriousness of the damage incurred, and the circumstances under which the right has been interfered with; this does not rule out a settlement agreement.

156. The list of the aforesaid actions is exemplary but other types of actions can be envisaged, such as the application for a preliminary ruling or an action to obtain evidence. The author may also request information from the customs authorities regarding the contents and scope of import of the goods, which:

(a) is a copy of the author's work or an audio or audiovisual record of such work;
(b) is to serve as a medium (empty medium) for the acquisition of such copy;
(c) is a device for making audio or audiovisual recordings or printed copies; or
(d) is a tool for the removal of copyright protection (e.g., decoder);

and inspect the customs documents in order to ascertain whether or not the import of such goods for the exploitation in the Czech Republic is justified, or to ascertain the data which may be decisive for exercising of the author's rights. The information may be also requested by the respective collective administrator as well as by a legal entity authorized to defend the authors' interests.

§11. Overlapping and Relation to Other Intellectual Property Laws

157. Copyright is, by its very nature, a personal right. The subject of the right to protect personality consists of individual components of human personality, while the subject of copyright is the specific manifestation of the author's personality. The main difference between the two subjects is that the right to protect personality has a general personality character – it means that it belongs to all natural persons alike. On the other hand, copyright may be classified as part of a group of special personality rights because its creation is subject to the implementation of a specific creative activity. Therefore, copyright can belong only to a person who carries out such activity as an author's. In the field of industrial rights, copyright is quite closely related to the right of invention or to the right to a trademark, while it is not ruled out that trademark may be also an author's work.

Chapter 2. Patents

§1. Sources: Legislation

158. Patents are regulated by Act no. 527/1990 Coll. providing for the inventions and innovative improvement proposals, as amended, and Decree no. 550/1990 Coll. on procedures in the matters of inventions and industrial patterns.

§2. Patentable Subject Matter

159. Patents are granted for the inventions that are new, resulting from inventive activities and usable in industries. The following items are not considered inventions:

(a) discoveries, scientific theories and mathematical methods;
(b) aesthetic creations;
(c) plans, rules and arrangements for the pursuit of intellectual activities, gaming or the pursuit of entrepreneurial activities, as well as computer programs;
(d) provision of information.

160. Methods of surgical or therapeutic treatment of human or animal body and diagnostic methods applied to human or animal body are also not considered inventions usable in industries. However, some products, in particular substances or mixtures to be used in these treatments and diagnostic methods, may serve as inventions.

161. Patents are not granted:

(a) for the inventions the use of which would be in conflict with public order or morals; this cannot be inferred only from the fact that the use of the invention is prohibited by law;
(b) for plant varieties and animal breeds or for basic biological methods of plant breeding or animal breeding; this provision does not apply to microbiological methods and products obtained by these methods.

162. An invention is new if it is not part of the state of the art. 'State of the art' means everything that was available to the public before the day as of which the priority right belongs to the applicant. The state of the art also means the contents of the applications for the inventions filed in the Czech Republic with earlier priority right, provided that they will be published on the day from which the priority right belongs to the applicant, or after that day. This also applies to the international applications for inventions with earlier priority right in which the Office is a designated authority, and the European patent applications with earlier priority rights for which the Czech Republic is the determined state.

163. The state of the art is not a publication of an invention which has occurred earlier than six months before the filing of the application for registration of the invention and which directly or indirectly results:

(a) from an apparent abuse with respect to the applicant or its legal predecessor;
(b) from the fact that the applicant or its legal predecessor exhibited the invention at an official or an officially recognized exhibition under an international agreement. In this case, the applicant is required to indicate upon filing the application that the invention was indeed exhibited and, within four months following the application filing date, prove by a certificate that the invention was exhibited in accordance with the international agreement.

164. An invention is a result of an inventive action unless it is apparent to a skilled person from the state of the art. The invention is deemed to be usable in an industry if the subject matter thereof may be manufactured or otherwise utilized in industrial, agricultural or other economic areas.

§3. Conditions of Patentability

165. The subject matter of the patent law is the results of technical creative activities that have the capacity to be granted patent protection. However, not all the technical solutions, which meet the legal requirements imposed upon a patentable invention, are eligible for patent protection.

166. The current Czech patent law does not contain a legal definition of an invention. It only sets out the terms and conditions an invention must meet in order to be granted a patent. Patents are granted to the inventions that are new, resulting from inventive activities and are usable in industry. It can be said that the law explicitly stipulates three conditions or, eventually, conceptual elements or patentability criteria. These are the novelty, inventive activities and industrial applicability.

167. These three terms represent an exhaustive list of conditions under which an invention is patentable. They all must always be met for the invention to be eligible for industrial protection. This also means that no further conditions can be imposed upon the evaluation of patentability of its technical solution.

168. An invention must fall within the scope of technical solutions for which the patent may be granted. It must not belong among the solutions which are not considered to be inventive and industrially applicable. At the same time, it must not belong among the items that are excluded from the scope of protection by law. The technical nature of a solution is a condition for granting patent protection. The invention must be of a technical nature, i.e., it must represent a technical contribution to the state of the art. This also applies if the problem itself does not have that nature. In terms of equipment, i.e., an object of technical nature, which solves a non-technical problem, such as how to effectively queue customers, there is no reason to exclude such solutions from patent protection.

169. The presumption of the technical nature of an invention cannot be considered to be fulfilled by the invention which, as claimed, may not rule out the use of technical means but also cover non-technical embodiments. The technical nature of an invention is an intrinsic property, which is independent on the actual contribution of the invention to the state of the art so that the potential of the claimed process aimed at the solution of a technical problem should be recognizable from the aspects of the process as is claimed. The fact that the result of the process is applicable to technical or industrial activities, or that the result is considered useful, practical or saleable, does not represent a sufficient condition for acknowledging the technical nature of such a result or the process itself.

§4. Formalities (Procedure for Granting and Obtaining Patent Protection)

170. An inventor or his legal successor has the right to a patent. The inventor is a person who created the invention by his own creative work. The patent award procedure is initiated by filing an application for the invention with the Office. The inventor must be clearly specified in the application. On request of the inventor, the Office shall not state his name when publishing the patent application and notification of the patent award.

171. An application for an invention must contain only one invention or a group of inventions mutually connected so that they form a single generic inventive idea. If the protection is requested in one application for a group of inventions, the requirement of uniformity of the invention is met if there is a technical relationship among the individual inventions, which relates to one or more identical or corresponding special technical features. The special technical features are understood as such technical features which determine the benefit of each one of the inventions contemplated to the state of the art.

172. The invention must be explained in the application clearly and comprehensively enough so that a skilled person could implement it. If the invention is an industrial production microorganism, it must be deposited in a public collection of cultures on the date on which the application has been granted the priority right.

173. If in doubt, the Office may invite the applicant to demonstrate the subject matter of the invention application or to prove the usability thereof in any other suitable fashion. If the applicant fails to do so, it is assumed that the subject matter of the application is not usable.

174. The priority right is established for the applicant upon filing the application. The applicant must claim the priority right resulting from an international agreement already in the application for the invention and prove it upon the invitation of the Office within a deadline stipulated by the Office; otherwise, the priority right would not be considered.

175. If a procedure has been instigated with the respective authority in a dispute regarding the right to a patent, the Office discontinues the application procedure. During that time, the statutory periods cease to run. The priority right is retained if the legitimate applicant files a motion for the continuation of the procedure within three months of the legal force of the decision regarding the patent right. The acts performed before the discontinuation of the procedure concerning the patent award are considered valid for further proceedings.

176. The Office shall rewrite the patent application, or the patent, respectively, to the person whom the court decides to be the inventor. The Office changes the applicant or the patent owner if the respective authority in the dispute over the patent right decides that the right belongs to another person.

177. The Office preliminarily examines the invention application to see whether or not it contains a subject matter which is apparently not patentable and whether or not it has shortcomings which prevent the publication thereof. If this is the case, the Office rejects the application. Before the application is rejected, the applicant must be given an opportunity to provide comments on the evidence upon which the decision is to be made.

178. If the application for an invention contains a subject matter which shows shortcomings preventing its publication, the Office invites the applicant to express its views of the facts and remove the shortcomings concerned. If the applicant fails to remove the shortcomings of the application, which prevent its publication, within a defined deadline, the Office discontinues the application procedure. In view of this, the applicant must be notified of the deadline.

179. The Office publishes the invention application upon the expiration of eighteen months following the creation of the priority right and announces the publication in the Bulletin. The application may be published before the deadline, provided that the applicant requests so no later than twelve months following the creation of the priority right. The Office publishes the invention application before the deadline expiration if the patent has already been granted to the invention. However, the Office will not publish the application before the expiration of the twelve-month period following the creation of the priority right without the consent of the applicant. Along with the invention application, the Office may publish a report on the state of the art (a research report) relating to the invention defined in the application.

180. Upon the publication of the application, anybody may file comments on the patentability of the subject matter thereof with the Office; the Office will consider the comments based on a full examination of the application. The persons who filed the comments do not become parties to the application procedure; however, the applicant must be notified of the comments.

181. The Office performs a full examination of the invention application to ascertain whether or not it meets the terms and conditions stipulated by law for the patent award. The Office performs the full examination of the invention application on request of the applicant or another person, or it may do so by virtue of office.

182. The request to conduct a full examination must be filed no later than thirty-six months following the filing date of the application and cannot be withdrawn. The Office proceeds with the full examination immediately after the application has been lodged. If the application for full examination has not been duly filed, or if the Office has not commenced the full examination of the application by virtue of office, the Office discontinues the application procedure.

183. If the conditions defined for the patent award have not been met, the Office rejects the application. Before the application is rejected, the applicant must be given an opportunity to express his views of the ground documents upon which the decision is to be made with respect to the application. If the applicant fails to remove the defects of the application, which prevent the patent award, within a defined period, the Office discontinues the procedure. In view of this, the applicant must be notified of the deadline.

184. If the subject matter of the invention application meets the conditions as defined, the Office grants the applicant the patent and the applicant becomes the owner thereof. The Office issues a patent deed to the patent owner stating the name of the inventor and containing a description of the invention and the patent claims and announces the patent award in the Bulletin. If there is more than one invention application with the identical subject matter thereof, only one patent can be granted.

§5. Ownership and Transfer (Assignment – Licenses)

185. If the rights to the same patent belong to several persons, the relations among them are governed by the general co-ownership regulations. Unless the co-owners agree otherwise, each co-owner has the right to make use of the invention.

186. Unless agreed otherwise, the consent of all co-owners is necessary for a valid conclusion of a licence agreement; each co-owner is entitled to make claims from the patent rights infringement separately.

187. The consent of all co-owners is also required for the transfer of a patent. A co-owner is entitled to transfer his share without the consent of the other co-owners only to another co-owner. A co-owner may transfer his share to a third party only in the case that none of the co-owners accepts a written offer of transfer within a one-month period.

188. The licence for use of a patent-protected invention is granted via a written agreement defined as a licence agreement. The licence agreement comes into effect towards third parties upon the registration thereof in the patent register. Patent is transferred by a written agreement which comes into effect towards third parties upon the registration thereof in the patent register.

189. The right may be assigned only upon a licence agreement. By the licence agreement, the provider grants the acquirer a licence to exercise the right to protect a topography within an agreed limited or unlimited scope and the acquirer undertakes to pay the provider a fee, unless the parties have agreed otherwise.

190. The licence comes into effect against third parties by the registration in the list of rights to protect topography managed by the Office. The acquirer is not obliged to make use of the licence unless the right's duration depends on the execution thereof.

191. In the event of an exclusive licence, the provider has no right to grant the same licence to a third party for as long as the exclusive licence is in force. Unless expressly agreed otherwise, the provider shall also refrain from exercising the right to which he has granted the exclusive licence.

192. If, during the force of the exclusive licence provided to the acquirer, the provider grants the licence to a third party without the acquirer's written consent, the licence will not be created. However, if a non-exclusive licence was granted prior to the provision of the exclusive licence, it will remain in force. If a non-exclusive licence has been granted, the provider is entitled to exercise the right to which he has granted the non-exclusive licence and grant it to a third party.

193. The licensee may grant a licence component fully or in part to a third party only if it has been agreed upon in the licence agreement. The licensee may assign the licence to a third party fully or in part only with the consent of the licence provider. The consent must be granted in the written form. Where a business establishment or a part thereof, which forms an independent unit of a business establishment, has been transferred, the consent of the provider with the licence assignment is requested only if it has been specifically agreed upon.

194. If a fee or the method of the determination thereof has not been agreed, the contract is nevertheless valid, provided that:

(a) the parties' negotiation regarding the conclusion of the contract implies their intention to execute a contract for value without determining the fee; in such a case, the acquirer shall pay the provider a standard fee which is customary at the time of the contract execution under similar contractual conditions and for such law; or
(b) the parties to the contract agree that the licence is granted free of charge.

195. If the fee has been agreed as depending on the proceeds from the use of the licence, the acquirer shall enable the provider to check the respective accounting entries or other documentation in order to ascertain the actual amount of the fee. Where the acquirer provides the information to the provider which is defined by the acquirer as confidential, the provider must not disclose it to any third party or use it for its own use at variance with the purpose for which it has been provided.

196. The acquirer shall conceal the documents and messages received from the provider and not disclose them to any third parties unless it is clear from the contract or from the nature of the documents and messages that the provider does not intend to keep them secret. A third party is not deemed to be an employee or a person who takes part in the provider's business unless bound by the non-disclosure obligation by the provider.

197. If the contract has been made for an indefinite period, the notice of termination comes into effect upon the expiration of one year from the end of a calendar month in which the notice of termination was delivered to the other party.

198. If the applicant or the patent owner declares before the Office that he grants the right to use the patent to anybody, the right to use the patent is created for any person who accepts the licence offer and informs the applicant or the patent owner about this fact in writing. The Office then records the licence offer in the patent register. The declaration of the licence offer cannot be undone. The establishment of the right to use the invention does not affect the patent owner's right to claim the price of the licence.

§6. Scope of Exclusive Rights

199. The patent owner has an exclusive right to make use of an invention, grant consent with the use of the invention to other persons or transfer the patent to other persons. The effects of the patent are established upon the day of announcement of the patent award in the Bulletin.

200. The applicant is entitled to a reasonable compensation from the person who was using the subject matter of the application after the publication thereof. The right to a reasonable compensation may be exercised as of the day on which the patent comes into effect. In the case of an international application for a patent to be granted in the Czech Republic, which is published upon an international agreement, the applicant is entitled to a reasonable compensation only after the publication of the translation thereof into Czech.

201. The scope of protection arising from a patent or an invention application is defined by the wording of the patent claims. Descriptions and drawings will be also used for the interpretation of the patent claims. The scope of protection for the period until the patent award arising from the invention application is defined by the wording of the patent claims contained in the published application. The patent, as granted or amended in the revocation proceedings, however, redefines the scope of protection arising from the invention application retroactively, unless the protection is thereby extended.

202. No one is entitled to do the following without the consent of the patent owner:

(a) to manufacture, offer, launch to market or use a product that is subject to a patent, or to import or store or otherwise handle the product for the purpose thereof;
(b) use a method that is the subject matter of a patent or offer the utilization method;
(c) to offer, launch to market, use or import or store a product for the purpose thereof which has been directly obtained via the method which forms the subject matter of a patent; whereas identical products are deemed to be obtained in the manner which is the subject matter of the patent if it is likely that the product was manufactured with the use of the patented method and the patent owner has not been able, despite reasonable effort, to define the production method actually applied, unless proven otherwise. When proving the opposite, the rights arising from trade secret protection must be saved.

203. Without the consent of a patent owner, no one can supply or offer to supply to another person but that authorized to use the patented invention any means relating to a substantial element of the patent serving in this respect to the implementation thereof, provided that it is obvious given the circumstances that the means have the capacity to implement the patented invention and are intended for the implementation thereof.

204. The patent owner has no right to prohibit third persons to handle a product that forms a subject matter of a protected invention if the product has been launched to market in the Czech Republic by the patent owner or with his consent unless there are reasons to extend the patent rights to the activities concerned.

205. The patent does not affect anyone who has used the invention before the establishment of the priority right independently of its originator or patent owner, or who has made demonstrable measures thereto. In the absence of agreement, the preceding user may claim at court to have the patent owner acknowledge his right.

206. The rights of a patent owner are not infringed if a protected invention is used:

(a) on ships of other countries that are members of the Paris Convention for the Protection of Industrial Property, which is binding upon the Czech Republic; in ship's body, machinery, ship equipment, devices and in other accessories, when these ships are temporarily or accidentally brought to the Czech Republic, provided that these items are used only for the needs of the ship;

(b) in the construction or operations of aircrafts or vehicles of the EU countries, or in parts of such aircraft or vehicles, if they are temporarily or accidentally brought to the Czech Republic;
(c) in the individual preparation of a drug at pharmacy based on a medical prescription, including the disposal of the drug prepared in this manner;
(d) in the course of activities carried out for non-commercial purposes;
(e) in the experimental activities carried out with the subject matter of the invention, including experiments and tests required by a special regulation prior to placing the drug on the market.

§7. Limitations and Exceptions to the Scope of Patent Protection: Compulsory Licences

207. If the patent owner does not use the invention at all and without a reason, or uses it insufficiently and failed to accept a due offer for the execution of a licence agreement within a reasonable deadline, the Office may grant a non-exclusive right to use the invention (compulsory licence) based on a justified request; the forced licence cannot be granted before the lapse of four years following the filing date of the invention application, or three years following the patent award, while the deadline which expires later rules. The forced licence may also be granted if there are grounds of jeopardy to an important public interest. The forced licence is registered in the patent register.

208. In its decision to grant a forced licence, the Office, considering the circumstances of the case, determines the conditions, scope and duration of the forced licence. The forced licence may be granted mostly for supplies to the domestic market. The forced licence cannot be transferred otherwise but as part of the transfer of a business establishment or a part thereof in which the entrepreneur concerned used the invention based on the forced licence. The forced licence holder may waive the right to use the invention at any time during the force thereof by filing a submission with the Office.

209. The Office revokes the forced licence or changes the conditions, scope or duration thereof on request of the patent holder in which he documents the change of the circumstances for granting the forced licence without the prospect of their future changes or that the forced licence holder has not used the licence for one year or fails to meet the terms stipulated upon granting the forced licence.

210. The fact of granting the forced licence does not affect the patent holder's right to claim the price of the licence. If the price of the licence has not been agreed upon by the parties involved, the court determines the price on request and with consideration of the significance of the invention and taking into account standard prices of contractual licences in a given industry.

§8. Duration of Protection: Maintenance and Termination of Patent Protection

211. A patent is good for twenty years following the filing date of the application for an invention. The owner is obliged to pay annual fees in order to keep the patent in force. A patent ceases to exist if:

(a) its force expires;
(b) the patent owner fails to pay the respective fees within the deadline to keep the patent in force;
(c) the patent owner surrenders the patent; in this case, the patent ceases to exist on a day on which the patent owner's written representation is served to the Office.

212. The Office revokes the patent if it is ascertained later:

(a) that the invention did not meet the patentability conditions;
(b) that the invention is not described in the patent clearly and sufficiently enough for a skilled person to implement it;
(c) that the subject matter of the patent exceeds the contents of the original application for the invention, or that the subject matter of the patents granted upon division of the application exceeds the contents of its original submission, or that the scope of protection arising from the patent has been extended;
(d) that the patent owner has no right to it; in this case, the Office revokes the patent upon the proposal of an authorized person.

If the grounds of the revocation apply only to a part of the patent, the patent is revoked only in that part. A partial revocation of the patent is carried out by changing its claims, description or drawings. The patent revocation has a retroactive effect from the date of the force thereof. An application for the patent revocation may also be filed after the patent has ceased to exist, provided that the applicant demonstrates a legal interest.

§9. Infringement and Remedies

213. In the case of unauthorized interference with the rights protected by this Act, except for the patent rights and additional protective certificates, a person whose right has been infringed may seek prohibition of the interference and the consequences thereof to be removed. If the interference caused damage, the aggrieved party has the right to compensation; it is to be compensated for the loss of property caused by the damaging event (the actual damage) and for what the aggrieved party would have achieved had the damaging event not occurred (lost profit). If the interference resulted in non-pecuniary damage, the aggrieved party has the right to a reasonable satisfaction, which may also consist in cash performance.

§10. Overlapping and Relation to Other Intellectual Property Laws

214. In the event of a conflict between a patent and a utility model, the law lays down, as an effect of the utility model, that the rights arising from the patent granted under an invention registration with a subsequent pre-emptive right, in the event of a conflict, may not be executed without the consent of the utility model owner. In this case the law puts the utility model owner in a stronger position against the patent owner that would illegitimately interfere with third-party rights without the consent.

Chapter 3. Utility Models

§1. Sources: Legislation

215. Utility models are regulated by Utility Models Act no. 478/1992 Coll., as amended, and Instruction no. 10/757/1992 providing the united form and requirements on applications for utility models.

§2. The Protection of Utility Models

216. Utility models protect the technical solutions that are new, go beyond mere professional skills and are usable in industries. The technical solution is new if it is not part of the state of the art. The state of the art is everything that was published prior to the day as of which the applicant of a utility model enjoys the priority right. The state of the art is not such disclosure of the results of work performed by the applicant or his legal predecessor that occurred in the past six months prior to the day on which the application for the utility model has been filed. The technical solution is usable in industries if it may be repeatedly used in economic activities.

217. Utility models do not cover, in particular:

(a) discoveries, scientific theories and mathematical methods;
(b) simple exterior modifications of products;
(c) plans, rules and methods of pursuing intellectual activity;
(d) computer programs;
(e) mere disclosure of information.

218. Utility models cannot protect:

(a) technical solutions in conflict with general interests, in particular with the principles of humanity and public moral;
(b) plant varieties and animal breeds, as well as biological reproductive materials;
(c) methods of production or work activity.

219. The originator of a utility model or his legal successor has the right to protection by the utility model. An originator is a person who created the utility model with his own creative work. Utility models are registered by the Industrial Property Office in the utility models register.

220. In order to register, an application for registration of a utility model must be filed. The application must contain only one technical solution or a group of solutions mutually connected so that they pursue a sole technical idea. Once the application is filed, the applicant enjoys the priority right. The applicant must claim the priority right which results from the Paris Convention for the Protection of Industrial Property already in the application and, at the same time, specify the date of filing the application from which he infers the priority right, application number and the state in which he filed the application or an authority with which he filed the application according to the international agreement.

221. A utility model becomes subject to protection upon the registration thereof in the register pursuant to the aforesaid Act. The Office issues a certificate documenting the utility model registration in the register to the applicant who thus becomes the owner of the utility model and announces the utility model registration in the Bulletin.

222. No one can manufacture, put into circulation or use a technical solution protected by the utility model in its economic activity without the consent of the utility model's owner. The utility model's owner is entitled to grant consent with the use of the technical solution protected by the utility model (licence) to other persons or transfer the utility model to other persons. In the case of a conflict, the rights resulting from the patent granted upon an application of the invention with a subsequent priority right cannot be exercised without the consent of the utility model's owner.

223. Utility model does not affect anybody who, prior to the acquisition of the priority right, used a technical solution protected by a utility model independently of the originator or the owner of the utility model, or who has made demonstrable measures to do so. In the absence of agreement, the previous user may claim at the court to have the utility model's owner acknowledge his right.

224. Utility model is good for four years of the filing date of the application, or the filing date of an earlier application for registration of an invention with an identical subject matter thereof. The Office may extend the force of the utility model's registration on request of its owner two times by three years each time.

225. Utility model ceases to exist if:

(a) the force expires;
(b) the owner surrenders it; in this case, the protection ceases to exist on the day on which the written representation of the utility model's owner is served to the Office.

On request of any person, the Office expunges utility model from the register:

(a) if the technical solution is not eligible for protection;
(b) if the subject matter of the utility model is already protected by a patent with effects in the Czech Republic, or by a utility model with an earlier priority right;
(c) if the subject matter of the utility model goes beyond the original utility model application.

226. The expungement of utility model has the effects as if the utility model has never been registered in the register. If the reasons for the expungement apply only to a part of the utility model, the utility model concerned is expunged only in that part. The utility model expungement may be exercised even after the utility model ceased to exist, provided that the applicant demonstrates a legal interest therein.

227. The Office keeps a register in which it records specified data on the applications for registration of utility models and registered utility models. An entity commits an offence by the unauthorized use of a technical solution protected by a utility model. A fine up to CZK 250,000 or a ban on activity may be imposed for the offence, or the publication of a decision on the offence may be also imposed if the offence is committed by a legal or an entrepreneurial entity. The offence is dealt with by the municipal office of a municipality with an extended jurisdiction.

Chapter 4. Trademarks

§1. Sources: Legislation

228. Trademarks are governed by Trademark Act no. 441/2003 Coll., as amended, public notice no. 97/2004 Coll. to implement the Trademark Act, and Act no. 634/2004 Coll. providing for administrative fees.

§2. Subject Matter of the Protection

229. In the Czech Republic, the trademarks enjoying protection are:

(a) registered in the Trademark Register administrated by the Industrial Property Office;
(b) have effect for the Czech Republic and are registered in a register administrated by the World Intellectual Property Organization based on an international application within the meaning of Madrid Agreement concerning the international registration of trademarks or the Protocol relating to Madrid Agreement;
(c) registered in a register administrated by the Office for Harmonization in the Internal Market (marks and models/designs) pursuant to the European Communities Council on EU trademark;
(d) generally known within the territory of the Czech Republic within the meaning of Article 6bis of the Paris Convention for the Protection of Industrial Property and Article 16 of the Agreement on Trade-Related Aspects of Intellectual Property Rights.

230. With consideration to the claimed priority right an earlier trademark is understood as:

(a) a registered trademark, if it has an earlier filing date:
 (1) a national trademark;
 (2) an international trademark;
 (3) an EC trademark;
(b) an EC trademark with respect to which a claim is made within the meaning of Article 34 of the Council Directive so as to enter the rights resulting from an earlier trademark, even if the owner of the earlier trademark surrendered the trademark or the trademark ceased to exist;
(c) a trademark under application pursuant to clauses (a) and (b), if it will be registered;
(d) a generally known trademark the protection of which was established prior to the filing date of the application of a subsequent trademark and continues to exist to that date.

231. The following signs will not be entered in the register:

(a) if it is not capable of a graphic representation, by words, including personal names, colours, drawings, letters, digits, numbers, a shape or a packaging of the product;
(b) which has no distinctive character;
(c) which consists solely of designations or data serving in trade for the determination of a kind, quality, quantity, purpose, value, geographical origin or date of manufacturing of goods or the provision of a service, or for the determination of other features thereof;
(d) which consists solely of the designations or data which has become customary in common language or in fair business practices;
(e) which consists solely of a shape resulting from the very nature of the product, or which is required for the achievement of a technical result, or which gives the product a substantial utility value;
(f) which conflicts with public order or morals;
(g) which could mislead the public, in particular in terms of the nature, quality or geographical origin of the product or service;
(h) which is applied for wines or spirits and contains a geographical origin without the wine or spirit being of that geographical origin;
(i) which contains an inscription enjoying protection pursuant to Article 6ter of the Paris Convention, the registration of which was not approved by the respective authorities;
(j) which contains other signs, emblems and coats of arms but those specified in Article 6ter of the Paris Convention if their use is a matter of special public interest unless the respective authority has given its consent with the registration thereof;
(k) which contains a sign of a highly symbolic value, especially a religious symbol;
(l) the use of which is contrary to the provisions of other legal regulation or conflicts with the obligations arising for the Czech Republic from international treaties;
(m) if it is obvious that the application for registration of a trademark has not been filed in good faith.

232. A sign which has no distinctive value, or which consists solely of signs or data serving in trade for the determination of a kind, quality, quantity, purpose, value, geographical origin or a date of manufacture of goods or the provision of a service, or for the designation of other properties thereof, or a sign which consists solely of the designations or data that have become customary in common language or in fair business practices, may be registered in the Trademark Register if the applicant proves that such a sign gained a distinctive value before the registration of the trademark by means of the use thereof in business with respect to the goods or services of the applicant for which the registration in the Trademark Register is being requested.

233. A sign will not be entered in the Trademark Register if it is identical to an earlier trademark, which has been applied or registered for another owner or applicant for identical goods or services; this does not apply if the owner or the applicant of the earlier trademark gives its written consent with the registration of the subsequent trademark in the Trademark Register.

234. The sign under application will not be registered in the Trademark Register based on objections filed against the trademark registration in the Trademark Register with the Office:

(a) by the owner of an earlier trademark if there is a likelihood of confusion thereof by the public due to the accordance or similarity with the earlier trademark and the accordance or similarity with the goods or services covered by the sign and the trademark applied for; the likelihood of confusion is also understood as the likelihood of association with an earlier trademark;
(b) by the owner of an earlier trademark that is identical to or similar with a sign under application, provided that such a sign is to be registered for the goods or services which may not be similar to those for which the earlier trademark has been registered but it is an older trademark with a good reputation in the Czech Republic and the use of the sign under application would unfairly capitalize on the distinctive features or a good name of the earlier trademark or be detrimental to them;
(c) by the owner of an earlier generally known trademark if there is a likelihood of confusion by the public due to the accordance or similarity with an earlier generally known trademark and the accordance or similarity of the goods and services covered by the sign applied for and the generally known trademark; the likelihood of confusion is also considered the likelihood of association with an earlier trademark;
(d) by the owner of an earlier generally known trademark that is identical to or similar with a sign applied for, provided that such a sign is to be registered for the goods and services which may not be similar to those covered by the earlier generally known and protected trademark but it concerns an earlier generally known trademark that enjoys a good reputation in the Czech Republic, provided that the use of the trademark in relation to such goods and services would evoke a relationship between the goods or services and the owner of the generally known trademark;
(e) by the owner of an earlier Community trademark that is identical to or similar with a sign applied for, provided that such a sign is to be registered for the goods or services which may not be similar to those covered by the registered earlier trademark but it concerns an earlier trademark which enjoys a good reputation within the territory of EU and the use of the sign applied for without a due reason would unfairly capitalize on the distinctive value or the good name of the earlier Community trademark or be detrimental to them;
(f) by the owner of a trademark registered in other member country of the Paris Convention or in a state that is a member of the World Trade Organization, provided that the application was filed by a representative, broker, agent or other person authorized to defend economic interests of the trademark owner pursuant to Article 6septies of the Paris Convention, on his behalf and without the consent of the owner, unless the agent duly substantiated his acts;

(g) by the user of an unregistered sign or another sign used in the course of business for identical or similar goods or services, which is identical to or similar with the sign applied for, provided that the sign does not have a local scope and the right thereto was created prior to the filing date of the application;
(h) by a natural entity whose right to the name and the protection of statements of personal nature may be affected by the sign applied for, or by the person authorized to exercise such personality protection rights;
(i) by a person who has the rights to author's work if the author's work could be affected using the sign applied for;
(j) by the owner of an earlier right resulting from other industrial property, provided that the industrial property rights may be affected by the use of the sign applied for;
(k) by a person whose rights are affected by the application which has not been filed in good faith.

I. Signs Which May Serve as Trademarks

235. Any sign capable of being represented graphically may be considered a trademark, in particular words, including personal names, colours, drawings, letters, figures, and a shape or a packaging of a product, if such a sign is capable of distinguishing the goods or services of one person from the goods or services of another.

II. Different Categories of Marks

236. The following signs may serve as trademarks:

(a) verbal inscriptions in standard script (words, names, a combination of words and digits, etc.);
(b) verbal inscriptions in a special graphical script;
(c) figurative signs (drawings);
(d) combined inscriptions consisting of a word and a drawing (logo);
(e) spatial (three-dimensional) inscriptions consisting of shapes of products or their packaging (e.g., bottles);
(f) a combination of a shape of a product or a packaging with words or drawings (e.g., a bottle bearing a label);
(g) a colour itself or a combination of colours.

237. In addition to verbal inscriptions in standard script, a trademark may be applied for according to the applicant's choice in a black-and-white or coloured design. In the case of a coloured trademark, the protection applies to the colours used and the arrangement thereof.

238. Depending on the nature of inscription, we distinguish the following trademarks:

(a) verbal (consisting of a word/words in a standard script);
(b) pictorial (consisting solely of a picture element);
(c) graphical (consisting of a graphically adjusted text without picture elements);
(d) combined (consisting of a combination of a text and a picture element);
(e) spatial (consisting of a shape of a product or a part thereof);
(f) consisting solely of a colour or a combination of colours.

§3. Conditions of Protection

239. A trademark has to be registered in the Trademark Register to have legal protection. And to be registered, it must meet two conditions. The trademark must be graphically depictable, i.e., can be expressed by a letter, figure, drawing, product shape, etc. Thus, the trademark must be visually perceivable. Moreover, it must be distinguishable, i.e., allow differentiating itself from products or services of the same type originating from different manufacturers or service providers.

240. In general, a registered trademark may not be constituted by a name that is common for the product or service in a given language or in fair trading or a denomination used in business to refer to product or service characteristics (type and descriptive designations). Thus, a trademark may not be, e.g., a specification of type, quality, quantity, purpose, value, territorial origin or production period of products or provision of a service.

241. These designations are not sufficiently distinguishable in relation to given products. The ability of the designation to be differentiated is assessed from the point of view of the common consumer, i.e., whether the common consumer would perceive such designation as a product description or a designation relating the product to a particular producer.

242. Descriptive designations, with regard to their general nature, may be used by anyone, since other tenderers may not be forbidden to refer to products of the same type using the same expressions. However, there are two exceptions from the impossibility to register type or descriptive designations. Such a designation may be used for products that have nothing in common with the product in terms of meaning. Moreover, such designations may be registered as trademarks if they have become common by means of practical usage for the products or services of the applicant and thus have acquired the ability to be distinguished in the particular case.

243. A trademark may not be a shape arising from the product nature or necessary for achieving a technical result or giving the product significant use value. Moreover, registration of a trademark may also not apply to symbols of state sovereignty, emblems and escutcheons, official testing, hallmark and warranty signs and other signs of high symbolic value, such as religious symbols.

§4. Formalities (Procedure for Obtaining Protection, Establishing and Maintaining Trademarks)

244. In order to register a trademark, an application must be filed with the Office. On the filing date, the priority right is created for the applicant over anyone who subsequently files an application for an identical or a similar trademark covering identical or similar goods or services.

245. The priority right, which is established by the Paris Convention, must be claimed by the applicant in the application and documented within three months following the filing date; otherwise, the Office will not grant it. The priority right may be claimed upon the application for the protection in an EU country of the Paris Convention or in a state which is a member of the World Trade Organization.

246. If the state in which the first filing is made is neither an EU country of the Paris Convention nor a member of the World Trade Organization, the priority right may be granted only upon the conditions of reciprocity. The deadline for proving the priority right cannot be extended and the lapse thereof remitted. On request of the applicant, the Office issues a receipt documenting that the priority right has been granted (receipt of priority).

247. If the sign applied for is not eligible for registration, the Office will reject the application. If the sign applied for is not eligible for registration only in part of the goods or services, the Office will reject the application within the respective extent. The information about the rejection of the application will be published by the Office in the Bulletin.

248. The Office will reject the application if the sign applied for contains elements of an earlier trademark applied for by or registered for another owner if those elements could cause confusion with the earlier trademark; the Office will not reject the application if the owner or the applicant of the earlier trademark grants a written consent with the registration of a subsequent trademark in the Trademark Register.

249. If the sign applied for contains an element which is devoid of any distinctive character, and if the retention of that element in the trademark could give rise to doubts as to the scope of protection, the applicant may limit the scope of protection with respect to the element of the sign applied for. The Office will publish the limitation of the scope of protection along with the application. If the conditions stipulated by this Act have been met, the Office will publish the application in the Bulletin.

250. Any person may submit written comments to the Office by the time the trademark is registered. The Office will consider the comments when deciding on the trademark registration in the Trademark Register. The person who submitted the comments does not become a party to the application procedure held before the Office. The applicant must be notified by the Office regarding the comments and the outcome of their examination and has the right to express his views within a specified deadline. The person who submitted the comments will be notified by the Office of the outcome of the examination thereof.

251. The application may be contested within three months following the publication of the application. The three-month term cannot be extended, and the lapse thereof cannot be remitted. The opposition must be filed in writing; it must contain the grounds thereof and be documented by evidence. The Office does not take into account any amendment to the opposition and the evidence submitted after the expiration of the deadline. Along with the opposition, the opponent must pay an administrative fee pursuant to a special regulation; if the administrative fee has not been paid, the opposition is deemed to have not been filed.

252. The Office will discontinue the opposition proceedings if the grounds for objection have lapsed and deliver the decision on the discontinuance of the proceedings to both the applicant and the opponent. If the Office does not discontinue the opposition proceedings or dismiss the opposition, it must notify the applicant of the contents thereof and stipulate a deadline in which the applicant may submit his statement. The Office may also invite the opponent and the applicant to try to reach an agreement regarding the opposition within a specified deadline. If the opposition is withdrawn, the Office will stop the opposition proceedings. If the applicant fails to provide his statement to the opposition within a specified deadline, the Office decides in accordance with the contents of the file.

253. If the Office ascertains that the trademark applied for does not infringe earlier third-party rights protected by law, it will dismiss the opposition. If, in the course of the opposition proceedings, the Office finds out that the trademark applied for does not meet the registration conditions only in terms of some goods and services for which the application has been filed, the Office dismisses the application within the scope of the goods or services in which the application fails to meet the registration conditions.

254. The Office serves the written decision on the dismissal of the application or the decision to dismiss the opposition to both the applicant and the opponent and publishes the information about the dismissal of the application, or the opposition, respectively, in the Bulletin.

255. Once the application has been filed, no changes can be made therein; in particular, the list of goods and services for which the application has been filed cannot be amended in any way. The application may be modified on request of the applicant only for the purpose of changing the name and surname, title, trade name and permanent residence address, registered office, or in order to correct errors in wording, transcription or any other obvious inaccuracies, provided that the change concerned brings the trademark data into compliance with the facts without changing the sign applied for in any substantial manner. If the modification concerns the sign applied for or the list of goods or services, and if the modifications are made after the publication of the application, the application will be republished as amended.

256. The applicant may withdraw the application at any time and the Office will discontinue the application procedure. The applicant may limit the scope of goods and services listed in the application at any time and the limitation cannot be withdrawn.

257. Up until the trademark registration in the Trademark Register, the applicant is entitled to divide the application to more than one product and service. The priority right from the original application will be retained also for the divided applications if they contain only the goods and services listed in the original application. The applicant is obliged to pay an administrative fee pursuant to a special regulation for as many applications as created due to the division of the original application.

258. If the application complies with the requirements of law and the application proceedings have not been discontinued and no opposition has been filed within a specified deadline or the opposition has been dismissed or the opposition procedure has been discontinued upon final and conclusive decision, the Office registers the trademark in the Trademark Register along with the date of registration, and issues a certificate of trademark registration to the owner. The trademark registration is then announced by the Office in the Bulletin. The trademark registration comes into effect on the date of the trademark registration in the Trademark Register.

§5. Ownership and Transfer (Assignment – Licenses)

259. Where the rights to the same trademark are shared by several persons, the relationships among them are governed by the co-ownership regulations. Unless the co-owners have agreed otherwise, each one of them has the right to use the trademark. Unless agreed otherwise, the consent of all co-owners is required in order to conclude a valid licence agreement; each co-owner is entitled to claim infringement of the trademark rights individually.

260. The transfer of a trademark is subject to the consent of all co-owners. A co-owner is entitled to transfer his share without the consent of other co-owners only to one of the other co-owners. A co-owner may transfer his share only in the case where none of the co-owners accepts his written offer of transfer within a one-month deadline.

261. A trademark may also be transferred upon written agreement. The transfer, or the passage, respectively, of a trademark comes into effect towards third parties upon the registration thereof in the Trademark Register; the acquirer of the trademark may perform acts towards the Office once the request for the registration of the transfer or the passage of the rights to the trademark has been delivered. Any contracting party is entitled to request the registration of the transfer or the passage of the rights in the Trademark Register; in the case of the passage, a legal successor of the original owner is entitled to do so.

262. The owner of a trademark registered in an EU country of the Paris Convention may file a petition with a court to determine the right to enter a change of the trademark owner if the trademark has been registered for an agent's name. The court dismisses the petition if the agent duly justifies his acts and substantiates the grounds thereof. Based on the final and conclusive decision of the court, the Office enters the change of the trademark owner on his request in the Trademark Register and announces this fact in the Bulletin of the Industrial Property Office.

263. A trademark may be the subject matter of the lien (security interest), enforcement of a decision or distraint, and may be included in the insolvency estate. The right to use a trademark may be granted upon a licence agreement for all goods or services for which the trademark has been registered, or for some of them. The licence may be granted as an exclusive or a non-exclusive one.

264. The trademark owner may invoke his rights to a trademark towards the licence acquirer who breached a provision of the licence agreement concerning the licence duration, the form in which the trademark may be used, the scope of goods or services for which the licence has been granted, the territory in which the trademark may be used, or the quality of goods and services manufactured or provided by the licence acquirer. The licence agreement comes into effect towards third parties upon the registration thereof in the Trademark Register.

265. The right may be assigned only upon a licence agreement. By the licence agreement, the provider grants the acquirer a licence to exercise the right to protect a topography within an agreed limited or unlimited scope and the acquirer undertakes to pay the provider a fee, unless the parties have agreed otherwise.

266. The licence comes into effect against third parties by the registration in the list of rights to protect topography managed by the Industrial Property Office. The acquirer is not obliged to make use of the licence unless the right's duration depends on the execution thereof.

267. In the event of an exclusive licence, the provider has no right to grant the same licence to a third party for as long as the exclusive licence is in force. Unless expressly agreed otherwise, the provider shall also refrain from exercising the right to which he has granted the exclusive licence.

268. If, during the force of the exclusive licence provided to the acquirer, the provider grants the licence to a third party without the acquirer's written consent, the licence will not be created. However, if a non-exclusive licence was granted prior to the provision of the exclusive licence, it will remain in force. If a non-exclusive licence has been granted, the provider is entitled to exercise the right to which he has granted the non-exclusive licence and grant it to a third party.

269. The licensee may grant a licence component fully or in part to a third party only if it has been agreed upon in the licence agreement. The licensee may assign the licence to a third party fully or in part only with the consent of the licence provider. The consent must be granted in the written form. Where a business establishment or a part thereof, which forms an independent unit of a business establishment, has been transferred, the consent of the provider with the licence assignment is requested only if it has been specifically agreed upon.

270. If a fee or the method of the determination thereof has not been agreed, the contract is nevertheless valid, provided that:

(a) the parties' negotiation regarding the conclusion of the contract implies their intention to execute a contract for value without determining the fee; in such a case, the acquirer shall pay the provider a standard fee which is customary at the time of the contract execution under similar contractual conditions and for such law; or
(b) the parties to the contract agree that the licence is granted free of charge.

271. If the fee has been agreed as depending on the proceeds from the use of the licence, the acquirer shall enable the provider to check the respective accounting entries or other documentation in order to ascertain the actual amount of the fee. Where the acquirer provides the information to the provider which is defined by the acquirer as confidential, the provider must not disclose it to any third party or use it for its own use at variance with the purpose for which it has been provided.

272. The acquirer shall conceal the documents and messages received from the provider and not disclose them to any third parties unless it is clear from the contract or from the nature of the documents and messages that the provider does not intend to keep them secret. A third party is not deemed to be an employee or a person who takes part in the provider's business unless bound by the non-disclosure obligation by the provider.

273. If the contract has been made for an indefinite period, the notice of termination comes into effect upon the expiration of one year from the end of a calendar month in which the notice of termination was delivered to the other party.

§6. Scope of Exclusive Rights

274. The trademark owner has an exclusive right to use a trademark in connection with the goods or services for which it is protected. The registered trademark owner proves his right by a copy of the entry thereof in the Trademark Register or by the registration certificate. Along with the trademark, the trademark owner is entitled to use the ® sign.

275. No one can use the following items without the consent of the trademark owner:

(a) a sign identical to a trademark for the goods or services which are identical to those for which the trademark has been registered;
(b) a sign in which there is a likelihood of confusion by the public, including the likelihood of association between the sign and a trademark, due to its accordance or similarity with the trademark, and the accordance or similarity of the goods or services labelled by the trademark and by the sign concerned;
(c) a sign identical to or similar with a trademark for the goods or services which may not be similar to those for which the trademark has been registered but it is a trademark which enjoys a good reputation in the Czech Republic and the use thereof would take an unfair advantage in the distinctiveness or the good name of the trademark, or be detrimental to them.

The following acts are considered the use of a trademark in trade:

(a) placing a sign to goods or its packaging;
(b) offering goods under a sign, introducing it to the market or storing for the purpose thereof, or offering or providing services under the sign concerned;
(c) importing or exporting goods under the sign concerned;
(d) using the sign concerned in commercial deeds and documents and in commercials.

276. If the reproduction of a registered trademark published in a dictionary, encyclopaedia or in a similar work implies that it is a generic title of goods or services, the trademark owner has the right to request that the publisher or the editor provides the trademark reproduction with an explanation stating that it is a trademark no later than upon the next publication of the work concerned.

§7. Limitations of the Scope of Trademark Protection

277. The trademark owner is not entitled to prohibit the use of the following by any third parties in trade:

(a) their name and surname, trade name or designation or address;
(b) data concerning the kind, quality, quantity, purpose, value, geographical origin, date of production of goods or provision of services or other features thereof;
(c) an inscription necessary to determine the purpose of goods or service, in particular in accessories or spare parts, provided that the use thereof is in compliance with business customs, morals and competition rules.

278. The trademark owner is obliged to tolerate the use of an identical or similar inscription in trade if the rights thereto had been created before the application was filed and the use thereof follows Czech law.

279. The trademark owner is not entitled to prohibit the use of the trademark for the goods launched on the Czech market along with the trademark by the owner or with his consent. The trademark owner is not entitled to prohibit the use of the trademark for the goods launched under the trademark on the market in a Member State of EU or in another state forming the European Economic Area by the owner or with his consent.

280. The owner of an earlier trademark is not entitled to request declaration of a subsequent identical or similar trademark void, or prevent its further use, if the owner tolerated the use thereof for five years following the date on which he learnt of the use, unless the application for registration of the subsequent trademark was not filed in good faith.

281. The owner of a subsequent trademark is not entitled to prohibit the use of an identical or a similar subsequent trademark or propose the declaration thereof void despite the fact that the owner of the earlier trademark could not claim his rights arising from the trademark any longer.

§8. Use Requirements

282. If the owner does not start duly use his trademark for the goods or services for which it has been registered within the period of five years following the registration thereof, or if the use of the trademark was interrupted continuously for at least five years, the trademark is cancelled by the Office, unless proper reasons exist for the non-use thereof.

283. The following acts are also considered due use of a trademark:

(a) the use of a trademark in the form that differs from the form in which the trademark has been registered by elements which do not change its distinctive character;
(b) the placement of a trademark on products or their packaging only for export purposes.

284. The use of a trademark under a licence agreement and the use of a collective trademark by a person entitled to use it is considered the owner's use. If an earlier trademark is not being used for all goods and services for which it has been registered, the existence thereof may constitute the grounds for the declaration of a subsequent trademark void only within the scope of the goods and services for which it has been used.

§9. Duration of Protection: Renewal – Termination

285. The registration of a trademark is good for ten years following the filing date of the application. Unless the owner applies for a renewal of the registration, the trademark ceases to exist. The trademark registration may always be renewed on request of the owner for another ten years. The request for the trademark registration renewal is filed not earlier than twelve months before the expiration of the registration force but no later than on the expiration date. The essential elements of the application for renewal of the trademark registration are stipulated by an implementing regulation. The deadline for filing the application for renewal of the registration cannot be extended and the lapse thereof cannot be remitted.

286. The application for the registration renewal may be filed within an additional six-month term following the expiration at the latest. The renewal of the trademark registration comes into force on the date on which the trademark registration expires; the Office records the registration renewal in the Trademark Register and publishes it in the Bulletin.

287. Upon written representation submitted to the Office, the owner can waive its rights to the trademark within the scope of all or some of the goods and services for which it has been registered; the representation comes into effect on the date of the delivery thereof to the Office and cannot be withdrawn. The Office enters the waiver of the rights to the trademark in the Trademark Register and announces it in the Bulletin.

288. Upon written representation submitted to the Office, the owner can also limit the scope of protection with respect to a trademark element. The Office decides on the limitation in view of the fulfilment of the conditions stipulated by this Act. The limitation of the scope of protection cannot be withdrawn.

289. The Office revokes a trademark in the proceedings instigated upon a third person's petition if:

(a) the trademark has not been duly used for five continuous years for the goods or services for which it has been registered and there are no proper reasons for not using it; the use which has been commenced or continued after the five-year period of non-use of the trademark within three months before filing the petition is not considered if the preparation for the commencement of the use or the continuation in the use occurred only once the owner learnt of the fact that a petition for the trademark revocation could be filed;
(b) the trademark has become a standard inscription in trade for the goods and services for which it has been registered due to acts or lack of acts of the owner thereof;
(c) the trademark may lead to confusion by the public in terms of the nature, quality or geographical origin of the goods or services for which it has been registered after the registration date due to the use by its owner or with his consent.

290. The Office revokes a trademark in the proceedings instigated upon a petition filed within six months following the legal effect of the court decision upon which the use of the trademark is considered unpermitted competition act. The deadline for filing the petition for the trademark revocation cannot be extended and the lapse thereof cannot be remitted.

291. In the proceedings instigated upon a petition filed by a third party or on the Office's own initiative, the Office declares a trademark void if it was registered in conflict with the law. This deficiency may be validated if, as a result of the use thereof, the trademark acquired, after its registration, a distinctive character for the goods or services for which it has been registered.

292. A trademark that was declared void is viewed as if it had never been registered. A trademark may be declared void even if the owner thereof surrendered it or if it ceased to exist by expiration.

293. The effects of revocation or invalidity of a trademark are not relevant for:

(a) any decisions passed with respect to an infringement of the trademark rights which came into legal force and was enforced prior to the legal force of a decision on the revocation or invalidity of the trademark;
(b) the contracts made prior to the legal force of a decision on the revocation or invalidity of a trademark within the scope of the performance provided on their basis before the legal force of this decision; however, it may be requested that the performance provided upon the contract is returned.

§10. Infringement and Remedies

294. A person commits an offence by unauthorized use of a trademark. A fine may be imposed for the offence up to CZK 250,000 or a ban on activity. If the offence is committed by a legal or an enterprising natural entity, the publication of the decision on the offence may be also imposed. The offence is heard by the municipal council of a municipality with an extended jurisdiction and cannot be dealt with by a warrant in situ.

§11. Overlapping and Relation to Other Intellectual Property Laws

295. A trademark right may conflict with the domain right. A domain name is solely an expression of a unique numeric identification. For this reason, a difference in a single attribute is enough for the domain to be sufficiently different from other, already registered domains, and therefore eligible for registration.

296. However, the right of other entities to their trademarks is an important question. A trademark can be used to protect the name of products and services. Domains are mostly registered and used in order to offer products or services, therefore there is no obstacle to them being registered as trademarks.

297. Assessment of the interchangeability of a domain and a trademark is a priority in the event of a conflict of these designations. If the trademark is not interchangeable with the domain, it may not be successfully applied towards the domain. Interchangeability is usually assessed in terms of the respective components of the designation (phonetic, visual and semantic), in terms of overall impression and in terms of similarity of products and services whose designations are assessed.

298. Domains must always be understood as purely verbal designations, i.e., without the specification of a particular graphic design, which may not even be applied. The above implies that solely a trademark whose distinguishability is also based on a verbal feature, interchangeable with the domain wording, may be applied against the domain. The more graphic features the trademark includes, the more these features must be considered and the lesser the degree of interchangeability of such a trademark with a purely verbal domain. The assessment always depends on the particular case, mostly in the uniqueness of the verbal features, which both the trademark and the domain are based on.

299. There is inverse proportionality between the similarity of the designations themselves and the similarity of the products and services they are used for. A higher degree of interchangeability of the designations themselves may counterbalance the lower degree of interchangeability of the products and services and vice versa; nevertheless, both the components must be present to a certain degree. For trademarks, the products and services are clear, since they are listed in the Trademark Register. For domains, the situation is different, there is no public register of products and services; however, the nature of domains is to enable products and services being offered to Internet users.

300. If the products and services offered under a domain were completely different from the trademark registration, such a domain would not be considered interchangeable with the trademark and therefore the trademark would not be applicable to the domain.

301. If an interchangeable domain is inactive, the trademark existence may not be used as an argument to support the statement that the domain was registered by another party in bad faith, although the party was aware of familiarity of the designation protected by the trademark and the domain corresponding to the trademark.

302. The issue of the relationship between domains and trademarks is affected by a very significant factor, namely the different territorial scope of both institutes. Whereas the territorial scope a domain as one of the significant pillars of the Internet in relation to users is practically unlimited, the territorial application of the trademark is clearly defined. In the event of a conflict between a national trademark and a national top level domain, such a trademark may clearly not be applied to the domain.

303. However, if the conflict is between a national trademark and a generic domain, the situation is not so clear-cut and additional criteria must be taken into account and used in the assessment of enforceability. Generally, the criterion of target consumers of the websites under the domain in question is decisive.

304. If the domain is protected by a trademark, there is no need to prove illegal conduct of the interchangeable domain holder, since it is sufficient to prove the existence of the trademark and similarity of products and services.

305. Unfair competition legislation is a private means to protect industrial property. It can be applied to nearly all cases of industrial law violation in ways that are often not optimally unsafe solely on special legal provisions of laws and regulations governing industrial property rights. This does not exclude its parallel application.

306. Typical conduct conflicting fair competition practice includes efforts to register a designation that is the same as or like a trademark that is already registered. Trademark law is a part of unfair competition law and in the event of a conflict substantive law prevails over the trademark law (i.e., formally acquired).

307. It may not be demanded that the trademark application itself constitutes unfair competition. The trademark application proceedings fall within the exclusive competence of the Office and the court may not interfere in any way since everyone has the right to present their proposals to an administrative authority and demand an administrative decision.

Chapter 5. Trade Names

§1. Sources: Legislation

308. Trade name law is a set of regulations governing trade name (also referred to as the corporate/business name), the rights to the trade name and the consequences of a breach thereof. Generally speaking, a summary of these regulations is included in the Civil Code (§423 an.), while more technical provisions regarding the creation and wording of a mandatory amendment, or the designations, respectively, are contained in the regulations applicable to individual corporations in the BCA. Other regulations only exceptionally define the form of a corporate branch; they more often define the form of a mandatory amendment, while at the same time they specify the exclusivity of such trade name only to a specific entity and prohibit the use of the defined form by other entities.

309. Company law is a part of private law; in particular, it may be classified as belonging to the intellectual property rights and, within the scope thereof, among the rights to a designation. Out of the rights to a designation, the trade name is the only one regulated by the CC, which is associated with a corporate obligation. Other rights to a designation are represented in other regulations. That being said, they are facultative and often of high material value. Company law is also governed by a number of public regulations of administrative or criminal law in the interest to protect the public and the public order.

§2. The Protection of Trade Names

310. The protection of trade names is not only based on the regulations of private law but also on public law. Of the private law regulations, it is primarily the CC and its provisions regarding unfair competition. The basic provision stipulates that anyone who, in the course of business, gets into a conflict with morals of competition due to his acting which could cause harm to other competitors or customers commits an act of unfair competition. Unfair competition is prohibited. It follows from the wording of the law that:

- unfair competition must take place in economic relations;
- is in conflict with competition morals; and
- can cause harm to other competitors or customers.

311. The unauthorized utilization of a trade name may be demonstrated particularly in the advertisement, misleading labelling of goods or services or parasiting on one's reputation. In the context of the facts of unfair competition, there is a pronounced position of the provision of section 2981 of the Civil Code regulating the likelihood of confusion.

312. The person whose right has been endangered or breached by unfair competition may request that the breaching party refrains from the act of unfair competition or removes the defective state. Such person may also request a reasonable satisfaction, compensation for damage and release of unfair enrichment. The request to refrain from such act may be applied with respect to a business corporation's trade name in two cases:

- somebody acts on behalf of a corporation prior to the incorporation thereof, while the trade name used is identical or similar (i.e., confusable) with the trade name of a corporation already registered in the commercial register;
- a corporation uses an abbreviation of a trade name instead of a registered trade name consisting of more than one word, and the abbreviation is identical or like a registered trade name owned by a different entity.

313. In the first case, removal of the defective state, which (above all) means the expungement of the confusable trade name from the commercial register, cannot be applied; in the latter case, it is also possible to seek removal of the defective state if the products or services distributed to the market have been labelled by the abbreviation concerned.

314. If the confusable trade name has already been registered in the commercial register, the person concerned may seek removal of the defective state, i.e., the expungement of the trade name or its modification so that the confusion would no longer be possible. In the given case, refraining from such an act is not applied as it would obstruct (legal) acting. Unless the parties agree otherwise, the damage is paid in cash; a reasonable satisfaction may also be of pecuniary nature.

315. As per the public law regulations, worth mentioning is at least the Trade Licensing Act, the Administrative Infractions Act and the Criminal Code. An entrepreneur is obliged to visibly attach its trade name, or the title or the name and surname and the identification number, to a building in which it operates its registered office, provided that it is different from its residence address; a foreign entity must visibly designate an organizational unit of a business establishment in the same way, provided that the foreign entity is the incorporator thereof. Otherwise, it commits an administrative infraction for which a fine up to CZK 5,000 may be imposed in an administrative hearing on a ticket.

316. An administrative infraction is committed by the person who breaches the obligation to use a trade name in business or the name and surname or a title in the case where the trade name does not exist. This administrative infraction is subject to a fine up to CZK 50,000 or a ban on the activity up to one year.

317. A term of imprisonment up to two years, a ban on the activity or confiscation of one's property or other property value shall be imposed upon the person who, for gaining economic benefit, unjustifiably uses a trade name or any other designation interchangeable with a trade name, or puts into circulation the goods or services unjustifiably labelled by an appellation of origin or a geographical indication or such a designation that is interchangeable with it, or, for this purpose, offers, mediates, produces, imports, exports or otherwise acquires or stores such goods or services for himself or for another person.

Chapter 6. Industrial Designs

§1. Sources: Legislation

318. Industrial designs are regulated by Act no. 207/2000 Coll. providing for the protection of industrial designs, as amended.

§2. Subject Matter of Protection

319. An industrial design is the appearance of a product or a part thereof, which consists particularly of the lines, contours, colours, shape, structure or materials of the article itself, or a decoration thereof.

§3. Conditions of Protection

320. An industrial design is eligible for the protection if it is new and has an individual character. An industrial design applied to a product, which represents a component of a composite product, or an industrial design embodied in such a product, is considered new and having an individual character only if:

(a) the component remains visible after the incorporation thereof into the composite product during standard use; and
(b) the visible features of the component themselves meet the requirement of novelty and individual character.

321. The standard use is understood as the use by an end user, except for the maintenance, service and repair works. An industrial design is deemed to be new unless an identical industrial design has been made available to the public before the filing date of the application or prior to the date of the priority right. Industrial designs are considered identical if their features differ only marginally.

322. An industrial design is of an individual nature if the overall impression it makes on an informed user differs from the overall impression made on such a user by an industrial design which was made available to the public before the filing date of the application or prior to the date of the priority right. When assessing the individual nature of an industrial design, the degree of freedom its designer had during the development thereof must be considered.

323. In assessing the eligibility of an industrial design for registration, the features that are predetermined by the technical function of the industrial design are not considered, nor are considered the features which must be necessarily reproduced in an exact shape and sizes so that the product in which the industrial design is embodied or applied to could be connected mechanically to another product or placed into another product or around it in order to make both products work.

324. The Office will not register an industrial design in the register if it in conflict with the principles of public order or with morals. The Office will not register an industrial design if an identical industrial design with an earlier priority right has been already registered in the Czech Republic.

§4. Formalities (Procedure for Granting and Obtaining Protection)

325. An application for registration of an industrial design is filed with the Office in writing. The Office will also accept an application for registration of the Community (industrial) design. In this case, the Office marks the date of the submission of the application and forwards it on to the Office for Harmonization in the Internal Market (marks and designs) within the next fourteen days thereafter.

326. If the application for registration of an industrial design is to establish the priority right, it must contain the following:

(a) an application for registration of the industrial design concerned in the register;
(b) name and surname, or a trade name, of the applicant, and permanent residence address or business establishment address if the applicant is a natural entity, and trade name or the company name and registered office address if the applicant is a legal entity;
(c) depiction of each industrial design applied for registration from which the nature of the industrial design could be clearly recognized, and which can be reproduced.

327. The application must also contain:

(a) the title of the industrial design;
(b) the designation of the product in which the industrial design is embodied or applied to, including its classification according to the respective classes of the international classification of industrial design;
(c) the name and surname of the designer or the applicant's statement that the designer surrenders the right to be named.

The application may also contain:

(a) a description explaining the depiction;
(b) an application for the postponement of the industrial design's publication.

328. The application may contain an application for registration of one industrial design (a simple industrial design application) or an application for registration of more than one industrial designs (bulk industrial design application). With the exception of decorative industrial designs, the bulk application may cover only those industrial designs which belong to one class of the international classification of industrial designs.

329. A bulk industrial design application must contain a list of industrial designs to be registered. The priority right is created in favour of the applicant on the filing date of the application for registration of an industrial design, provided that the application contains all the essential elements. The applicant must claim the priority right resulting from the Paris Convention within one month of the application filing date, and, on request of the Office, prove the priority right within a deadline specified by the Office; otherwise, the Office will not take the priority right into account.

330. The priority right may be claimed upon an industrial design application requesting protection in a Member State of the Paris Convention or in a state that is a member of the World Trade Organization; if the state in which the first industrial design application has been filed is not a party to the Paris Convention or a member of the World Trade Organization, the priority right may be granted only upon the condition of reciprocity.

331. The Office shall examine the application and, if the application fails to contain all essential elements, the Office invites the applicant to remove the shortcomings within a specified deadline. Should the applicant fail to do so, the Office would discontinue the application procedure.

332. The applicant is entitled to divide a bulk industrial design application until it is registered. The priority right from the original application will be preserved also for the divided applications if they contain only the industrial designs specified in the original application.

333. If the subject matter of an application is not an industrial design, or if the industrial design in question fails to meet the requirements imposed upon it, the Office shall dismiss the application. An industrial design application will be also rejected due to a collision with an earlier identical industrial design with effects in the Czech Republic, which was made available to the public after the application filing date, or after the date of the priority right. Before the application is rejected, the applicant must be given an opportunity to provide his statement to the grounds upon which the application is to be rejected.

334. If nothing prevents it then, the Office shall register an industrial design in the register and issue a certificate of registration to the applicant. Along with the registration of the industrial design in the register, the Office shall publish the registered industrial design and announce the registration thereof in the Bulletin of the Industrial Property Office.

335. If the applicant requested in the application a postponement of the industrial design publication not exceeding thirty months following the application filing date or the date of the priority right, the Office shall publish the industrial design after the expiration of the requested period. Along with the notification of the registration, the Office shall also announce the postponement of the industrial design publication.

336. Court proceedings due to infringement of the rights arising from a registered industrial design that has not been published yet may be instigated only under the condition that the information contained in the register and in the file relating to the industrial design application has been communicated to the person against whom the action has been brought.

337. A disquisition may be filed against the Office's decision, except for a decision to waive a lapse of a deadline, within one month of the delivery of the disquisition. The disquisition is subject to a decision of the Chairman of the Office based on a proposal by an expert committee appointed by the Chairman.

§5. Ownership and Transfer (Assignment – Licenses)

338. If the rights arising from a registered industrial design belong to several persons, the relationships among them are governed by the general regulations providing for co-ownership. Unless co-owners agree otherwise, each one of them has the right to make use of the industrial design concerned.

339. Unless agreed otherwise, the consent of all co-owners is required for the conclusion of a licence agreement. Each co-owner is entitled to assert claims related to infringement or imperilment of the rights to an industrial design individually.

340. The consent of all co-owners is required for the transfer of the rights to a registered industrial design. Without the consent of other co-owners, a co-owner is entitled to transfer his share only to another co-owner. A co-owner may transfer his share to a third party only in the case where none of the co-owners accepted his offer to transfer his share within a one-month period.

341. The rights to an industrial design are transferred by a written agreement which comes into effect towards third parties upon the registration thereof in the Industrial Designs Register. Until the transfer is marked in the Industrial Designs Register, the legal successor cannot claim the rights arising from the registered industrial design against any third parties.

342. A registered industrial design may be subject to the lien. The lien is created upon the registration thereof in the Industrial Designs Register. A registered industrial design may also be subject to the execution of a decision.

343. The consent (a licence) to use a registered industrial design is granted upon a licence agreement. The licence may be exclusive or non-exclusive. The licence agreement comes into effect towards third parties upon the registration thereof in 'the Industrial Design Register'.

344. The right may be assigned only upon a licence agreement. By the licence agreement, the provider grants the acquirer a licence to exercise the right to protect a topography within an agreed limited or unlimited scope and the acquirer undertakes to pay the provider a fee, unless the parties have agreed otherwise.

345. The licence comes into effect against third parties by the registration in the list of rights to protect topography managed by the Industrial Property Office. The acquirer is not obliged to make use of the licence unless the right's duration depends on the execution thereof.

346. In the event of an exclusive licence, the provider has no right to grant the same licence to a third party for as long as the exclusive licence is in force. Unless expressly agreed otherwise, the provider shall also refrain from exercising the right to which he has granted the exclusive licence.

347. If, during the force of the exclusive licence provided to the acquirer, the provider grants the licence to a third party without the acquirer's written consent, the licence will not be created. However, if a non-exclusive licence was granted prior to the provision of the exclusive licence, it will remain in force. If a non-exclusive licence has been granted, the provider is entitled to exercise the right to which he has granted the non-exclusive licence and grant it to a third party.

348. The licensee may grant a licence component fully or in part to a third party only if it has been agreed upon in the licence agreement. The licensee may assign the licence to a third party fully or in part only with the consent of the licence provider. The consent must be granted in the written form. Where a business establishment or a part thereof, which forms an independent unit of a business establishment, has been transferred, the consent of the provider with the licence assignment is requested only if it has been specifically agreed upon.

349. If a fee or the method of the determination thereof has not been agreed, the contract is nevertheless valid, provided that:

(a) the parties' negotiation regarding the conclusion of the contract implies their intention to execute a contract for value without determining the fee; in such a case, the acquirer shall pay the provider a standard fee which is customary at the time of the contract execution under similar contractual conditions and for such law; or
(b) the parties to the contract agree that the licence is granted free of charge.

350. If the fee has been agreed as depending on the proceeds from the use of the licence, the acquirer shall enable the provider to check the respective accounting entries or other documentation in order to ascertain the actual amount of the fee. Where the acquirer provides the information to the provider which is defined by the acquirer as confidential, the provider must not disclose it to any third party or use it for its own use at variance with the purpose for which it has been provided.

351. The acquirer shall conceal the documents and messages received from the provider and not disclose them to any third parties unless it is clear from the contract or from the nature of the documents and messages that the provider does not intend to keep them secret. A third party is not deemed to be an employee or a person who takes part in the provider's business unless bound by the non-disclosure obligation by the provider.

352. If the contract has been made for an indefinite period, the notice of termination comes into effect upon the expiration of one year from the end of a calendar month in which the notice of termination was delivered to the other party.

§6. Scope of Exclusive Rights

353. The registration of an industrial design provides its owner with an exclusive right to use the industrial design, prevent third parties from using it without his consent, give his consent with the use of the industrial design to other persons or transfer the industrial design to them. The use of an industrial design means, in particular, the production, offering, placing on the market, importing, exporting or using the product in which the industrial design is embodied or applied to, or storing such product for the aforesaid purposes.

354. The rights arising from a registered industrial design come into force on the filing date of the application. If the industrial design has not been published yet, its owner may exercise the rights arising from the registration towards third parties only if the industrial design is not being used in good faith.

355. The scope of protection is subject to the representation of the industrial design as it is registered in the Industrial Designs Register, with the exception of characters that are predetermined by the technical function of the industrial design, or characters which must necessarily be reproduced in an exact shape and dimensions so that the product in which the industrial design is embodied or applied to could be connected mechanically with another product, or placed into another product, around it or against it so that both products could fulfil their function. The scope of protection resulting from the registration of an industrial design covers every industrial design which does not give an informed user a different overall impression.

§7. Limitations of the Scope of Protection

356. The rights arising from a registered industrial design do not apply to:

(a) acts of third parties carried out for non-commercial purposes;
(b) acts of third parties carried out for experimental purposes;
(c) acts of third parties consisting in a reproduction for quoting or teaching purposes, provided that such acts are compatible with fair business practices and

are not unreasonably at the expense of the proper use of the industrial design concerned, and their source is always properly stated.

The rights arising from a registered industrial design also do not apply to:

(a) equipment of ships and aircrafts registered in another country in the case that they are temporarily brought in the Czech Republic;
(b) import of spare parts and accessories in the Czech Republic for the purpose of repair of such a transportation means;
(c) execution of repairs of such transportation means.

357. The rights arising from a registered industrial design do not apply to the handling of a product in which a protected industrial design is embodied or applied to, provided that the product concerned has been placed on the market in the Czech Republic by the owner of the registered industrial design or with his consent.

358. The rights arising from a registered industrial design do not apply to the handling of a product in which a protected industrial design is embodied or applied to, provided that the product concerned has been placed on the market within EU or in another state that is part of the European Economic Area by the owner of the registered industrial design or with his consent.

359. The rights arising from a registered industrial design do not affect any third parties which can prove that they commenced using an industrial design falling within the scope of protection of a registered industrial design in the Czech Republic before the filing date of the application or prior to the date of the priority right, provided that the used industrial design was created independently of the registered industrial design, or that the parties made serious preparations for the purpose thereof. Such persons are entitled to use the industrial design in their entrepreneurial activity in which the previous use was carried out or was under preparation. The right of a previous user cannot be transferred separately from a business establishment or a part thereof to which it relates.

360. The right from a registered industrial design extinguishes if:

(a) the protection period expires;
(b) the industrial design owner waives it; in such a case, the right extinguishes if this fact has been marked in the Industrial Designs Register. If the industrial design is subject to any third-party rights, the Office marks the extinction once it receives evidence from the industrial design owner that the third parties have been informed about the owner's intention.

361. The Office expunges a registered industrial design from the Industrial Designs Register:

(a) if the industrial design does not comply with the concept of an industrial design;
(b) if the industrial design does not meet the requirements stipulated by law;
(c) if the owner thereof does not have the right to it;
(d) if the industrial design has been already applied for or protected with effects in the Czech Republic as an earlier industrial design but it was made available to the public after the date of the priority right of a challenged industrial design;
(e) if a distinctive designation is used in an industrial design which provides the owner of the designation with the right to prohibit such use before the creation of the priority right of the industrial design;
(f) if the industrial design represents unauthorized use of a work protected by copyright;
(g) if the industrial design constitutes an abuse of any elements listed under Article 6ter of the Paris Convention concerning the protection of industrial property or other symbolic signs, flags and coats of arms not covered by Article 6ter of the Paris Convention, which, however, represent a special public interest in the respective Member State.

362. The expungement of a registered industrial design from the Industrial Designs Register has the same effect as if the industrial design has never been registered. An application for the expungement of a registered industrial design must be filed with the Office in writing. The application must be duly substantiated and the evidence on which the application is based must be submitted at the same time. The grounds of the expungement, including the evidence claimed, cannot be changed or amended. The Office will invite the owner of the industrial design to provide a statement on the application within a specified term. If the owner of the industrial design fails to provide his statement on the application for the expungement, it does not represent any obstacle for the Office to decide on the expungement application.

§8. Duration of Protection

363. The protection of a registered industrial design lasts for five years following the filing date of the application. The owner of a registered industrial design may renew the protection repeatedly by another five years each time up to the total period of twenty-five years following the filing date of the application for registration of an industrial design. An application for renewal may be filed in the course of the last year of the respective five-year period but no later than on the day that corresponds in number and name with the filing date of the application.

364. If the application is not filed, the owner is entitled to do so within six months following the date on which it was due to be filed at the latest. If the application is not filed even within the additional period, the protection of the industrial design concerned terminates on the date on which it was due to be filed at the latest.

365. The rights of third parties who have begun to use an industrial design or made serious and effective preparations to do so in good faith after the idle expiration of the deadline for filing the application for the renewal of protection of industrial design are not affected by the renewal exercised based on an additional application for renewal.

§9. Infringement and Remedies

366. A person commits an offence by the unauthorized use of an industrial design. For this offence, a fine up to CZK 250,000 or a ban on activity may be imposed. If the offence is committed by a legal or natural person carrying out an enterprise, the publication of a decision on the offence may be also imposed. The offence is heard by the municipal council of a municipality with an extended jurisdiction and cannot be dealt with by a warrant in situ.

367. The disputes concerning the determination of the right to an industrial design are decided by courts. An action for the determination of a legitimate applicant, or an owner of a registered industrial design, may be filed within two years following the registration of the industrial design in the Industrial Designs Register; this does not apply if the applicant failed to act in good faith.

368. The Office shall, upon an application, remove protection from the owner of a registered industrial design if it ascertains from a court decision that the owner did not have the right to the industrial design in question. The application for the removal of protection may be filed only by the person or a legal successor thereof who, according to the court's decision, has the right to the industrial design concerned.

369. On request of the person who has the right to protection of an industrial design, the Office shall register that person as the owner of the industrial design. The application for change of the owner of the industrial design must be substantiated by the court's decision. If the application for change of the owner of an industrial design is not filed, the Office expunges the industrial design from the Industrial Designs Register by virtue of office.

370. Once the legitimate owner is registered in the Industrial Designs Register, the licences and other rights granted by the previously registered owner of an industrial design extinguish. If the originally registered owner of an industrial design or a third party who acquired the licence to use the industrial design from the owner used or made serious preparation for the use of the industrial design before the action was filed, they may continue using the industrial design, provided that they request the execution of a non-exclusive licence under standard conditions; the request must be filed within two months following the day on which the legitimate owner of the industrial design informed them of the change of the industrial design's owner. This does not apply if the originally registered owner of the industrial design, or a third party who acquired the licence from the owner, failed to act in good faith.

§10. Overlapping and Relation to Other Intellectual Property Laws

371. Both the Copyright Act and the Act on Industrial Designs lay down the principle of mutual concurrency of both legal regimes. Copyright protection does not rule out protection laid down in other laws and regulations.

372. For copyright works, the applicable provisions of the Copyright Act assume that the subject of the protection must be a unique result of intellectual activity and is not solely of an individual nature. Unique subjects form a subset of subjects of individual nature. Copyright law does not automatically protect identical subjects of protection like the industrial design law.

373. Copyright protection starts at the moment of the work portrayal in an objectively perceivable form, whereas the protection of industrial designs generally starts only by registration. This means that copyright protection will always precede the protection of industrial designs, since it starts automatically, without the need of a formal record.

374. The author of a copyrighted work has the right to use the work, which means, among other things, to register the work as industrial design. In the event of concurrence, the author will always be the originator. However, the applicant may be a person different from the author, e.g., an employer or client.

375. The author has the right to use (register) their work both in the form of the original work and in the form of a derived (i.e., modified) work. It is obvious that in the event of concurrence, the work (or material medium) will be modified frequently since, in the course of industrial production of an item protected by copyright law, the issue of the necessary modification in terms of operation or marketing will need to be addressed. Another question to be dealt with will come upon the industrial design application when certain features (attributes) of the particular copyright work will have to be modified in order for the product to fulfil its technical function. Thus the depiction of the industrial design in the register may differ from the original work.

376. A mutual conflict between the rights arising from trademark registration and the rights arising from the industrial design registration must be resolved on a priority basis. An industrial design is protected only as new. However, this rule does not apply to trademarks; to the contrary, the law explicitly assumes the trademark was used in business before the application date.

Chapter 7. Plant Variety Protection

§1. Sources: Legislation

377. This area is regulated by Act no. 408/2000 Coll. providing for the plant variety protection, as amended.

§2. Subject Matter of Protection

378. The subject of protection is the varieties of plants defined by the International Convention for the Protection of New Varieties of Plants. The protection establishes the rights and obligations related to plant varieties as defined in the decision of the Institute.

§3. Conditions of Protection

379. The protective rights may be granted to varieties of all genera and species of plants, including their hybrids. The protective rights may be granted to a variety which meets the conditions of:

(a) novelty;
(b) distinctiveness;
(c) uniformity; and
(d) stability.

380. The protective rights are granted and the obligations associated therewith are stipulated by the Institute. The protective rights cannot be granted to a variety which has been granted the Community plant variety right.

381. A variety meets the condition of novelty if, at the date of the application for the protective rights, its propagation material or the harvesting material of the variety has not been sold by the cultivator, or with his consent, or otherwise provided for use by other persons:

(a) in the Czech Republic for more than one year before the date of application;
(b) outside the Czech Republic for more than four years before the date of application or, in the case of a woody plant or vine plant, for more than six years before the date of application.

Providing for use by other persons is not considered:

(a) if the cultivator sells to another person or otherwise provides another person with the propagation or harvested material without designating the variety, which was obtained from the plants grown for research purposes or for the creation of other varieties, and which is not used for further propagation; or

(b) if the cultivator exhibited the variety at an international exhibition pursuant to the international agreement.

382. The variety meets the condition of distinctiveness if it clearly differs from any other variety, which is generally known on the date of application for the protective rights, by at least one sign resulting from the variety's genotype or a combination of genotypes. The varieties that are considered generally known are those that are:

(a) protected in the Czech Republic or abroad;
(b) registered in an official list in the Czech Republic or in a similar list abroad;
(c) for which an application for the protective rights or an application for registration in an official list has been filed in the Czech Republic, provided that the application will be taken into account;
(d) for which an application for the protective rights or an application for registration in an official list has been filed abroad, provided that the application will be taken into account; or
(e) offered for sale or available for sale in the Czech Republic or abroad.

383. The same name of a variety used in an EU Member State or by another EU member must be used for the same variety in the Czech Republic. The 'variety names' set forth are not admissible:

(a) those consisting only of numbers, except where such a designation represents an established practice for the designation of varieties;
(b) those identical to or interchangeable with a name used for another variety of the same or relating kind in the Czech Republic, in another EU Member State or in another member of the EU;
(c) those evoking erroneous ideas about the value, properties or origin of variety or the identity of the cultivator;
(d) those that are identical to or interchangeable with a trademark, appellation of origin or a geographical indication for the same or similar goods, or those otherwise infringing the rights or protected interests of other persons;
(e) inappropriate in terms of language.

§4. Formalities (Procedure for Grant and Obtaining Protection)

384. A cultivator who is the citizen of the Czech Republic, another EU Member State or another EU member, or a person residing in the Czech Republic, another EU Member State or another EU member, is entitled to file an application for the protective rights to a variety. The application may be filed jointly by several applicants.

385. The application may be also filed by a natural entity who is the citizen of a state or is residing in a state which provides the persons from an EU Member State or an EU member with a similar protection for the varieties of the same botanical classification; the application may also be filed by a legal entity with its registered office in such a state.

386. The application must contain the following data:

(a) the name, or names, surname and permanent residence address of the applicant, if he is a Czech citizen, or his residence address in another Member State or a state which is an EU member, if the applicant is a citizen of another Member State or a state which is a member of the EU, or a trade name or a title, registered office or organizational unit's address in the Czech Republic and a specification of legal form if the applicant is a legal entity;
(b) both Latin and Czech name of the variety, or another specification of a botanical classification;
(c) proposal of a name or a preliminary variety designation;
(d) details of all previous applications for the protective rights filed in connection with the variety concerned;
(e) details of the previous use of the variety;
(f) description of the variety.

387. The protective rights to a variety may be granted to a cultivator who filed an application for the protective rights with the Institute. If more than one cultivator participates in the creation of a variety, they share the protective rights to the variety equally unless they have agreed otherwise in a written contract. The Institute enters the application into the list of applications in the order in which it has been received.

388. Where more than one application is filed with the Institute for the protective rights to an identical variety, such rights may be granted only to the applicant who first filed the application; at the same time, upon the fulfilment of the conditions set forth herein, the priority right arising from an earlier filing of the application in any EU Member State must be acknowledged.

389. If the applicant submits an application in another EU Member State before submitting it in the Czech Republic, the applicant enjoys the priority right to the same variety after filing the application in the Czech Republic twelve months following the application filed in another EU Member State, provided that the applicant claimed the priority right in the application filed with the Institute. The Institute will not consider the priority right if the applicant fails to submit an authenticated copy of the earlier application he filed in another EU Member State within three months thereafter. An application for the Community plant variety right may be also filed through the Institute. The Institute then specifies the date of submission in the application.

390. The Institute shall publish the following data in the Bulletin of the Central Institute for Supervising and Testing in Agriculture:

(a) notification of the submitted applications in the order according to the dates of submission, and details of the applicant;
(b) a change of the proposed variety name or a proposal of a variety name where the application contained only a preliminary designation of the variety concerned.

Anybody is entitled to file opposition with the Institute against:

(a) a submitted application; the opposition must not be filed later than by the date of the decision passed by the Institute;
(b) a proposal of a variety name no later than three months following the publication thereof in the Bulletin of the Central Institute for Supervising and Testing in Agriculture.

391. The opposition may be filed only on the grounds that the conditions stipulated by law have not been met, or there is an obstacle to the admissibility of the proposed name. The opposition must be submitted in writing and must contain the following data:

(a) the name, or name, surname and residence address of a natural person, or a trade name, or a title, registered address, or address of an organizational unit in the Czech Republic, and the specification of legal form of the legal entity who submits the opposition;
(b) identification of the subject matter of the opposition;
(c) grounds of the opposition, including submission of evidence substantiating the merits of the opposition.

392. The Institute shall settle the opposition by the date of its decision at the latest. The Institute shall examine whether or not the variety complies with the requirements of novelty, distinctiveness, uniformity and stability, and whether or not the proposed name meets the conditions stipulated by law. The distinctiveness, uniformity and stability are determined by the field and laboratory tests. When assessing varieties, the Institute may use the results of the tests of distinctiveness, uniformity and stability ascertained by expert laboratories abroad.

393. The applicant is obliged:

(a) to supply the variety material necessary for the examination thereof to the Institute free of charge and within a reasonable deadline stipulated by the Institute;
(b) to reimburse the Institute for the necessary costs of professional activities associated with the procedure for granting the protective rights.

394. It the conditions stipulated by this Act have been met, the Institute shall grant the applicant the protective rights to the variety and approve the proposal of the variety name by issuing a cultivator's certificate. The cultivator's certificate contains the designation of the kind of variety, the name of the variety, and the name, surname, residence address or registered office address, seat and legal form of the cultivator's rights holder. The cultivator's certificate also includes a description of the variety based on the results of the distinctiveness, uniformity and stability tests.

§5. Ownership and Transfer (Assignment – Licenses)

395. The cultivator's right holder may assign the protective rights to a protected variety by written contract to another person. If the protective rights to the same protected variety belong to several persons, the share in the rights may be assigned to any co-holder of the cultivator's rights without the consent of the other co-holders; a co-holder may assign his share to a third party only in the case that none of the other co-holders accepts his written offer of assignment within one month following the delivery thereof.

396. The contract to assign the protective rights to a protected variety or the contract to assign a share in the protective rights to a protected variety comes into effect on the date of registration thereof in the register of protected varieties managed by the Institute.

397. The protective right holder may grant his consent with the use of a protected variety to another person. The licence is granted upon a written agreement containing a provision concerning the price of the licence.

398. The right may be assigned only upon a licence agreement. By the licence agreement, the provider grants the acquirer a licence to exercise the right to protect a topography within an agreed limited or unlimited scope and the acquirer undertakes to pay the provider a fee, unless the parties have agreed otherwise.

399. The licence comes into effect against third parties by the registration in the list of rights to protect topography managed by the Industrial Property Office. The acquirer is not obliged to make use of the licence unless the right's duration depends on the execution thereof.

400. In the event of an exclusive licence, the provider has no right to grant the same licence to a third party for as long as the exclusive licence is in force. Unless expressly agreed otherwise, the provider shall also refrain from exercising the right to which he has granted the exclusive licence.

401. If, during the force of the exclusive licence provided to the acquirer, the provider grants the licence to a third party without the acquirer's written consent, the licence will not be created. However, if a non-exclusive licence was granted prior to the provision of the exclusive licence, it will remain in force. If a non-exclusive licence has been granted, the provider is entitled to exercise the right to which he has granted the non-exclusive licence and grant it to a third party.

402. The licensee may grant a licence component fully or in part to a third party only if it has been agreed upon in the licence agreement. The licensee may assign the licence to a third party fully or in part only with the consent of the licence provider. The consent must be granted in the written form. Where a business establishment or a part thereof, which forms an independent unit of a business establishment, has been transferred, the consent of the provider with the licence assignment is requested only if it has been specifically agreed upon.

403. If a fee or the method of the determination thereof has not been agreed, the contract is nevertheless valid, provided that:

(a) the parties' negotiation regarding the conclusion of the contract implies their intention to execute a contract for value without determining the fee; in such a case, the acquirer shall pay the provider a standard fee which is customary at the time of the contract execution under similar contractual conditions and for such law; or
(b) the parties to the contract agree that the licence is granted free of charge.

404. If the fee has been agreed as depending on the proceeds from the use of the licence, the acquirer shall enable the provider to check the respective accounting entries or other documentation in order to ascertain the actual amount of the fee. Where the acquirer provides the information to the provider which is defined by the acquirer as confidential, the provider must not disclose it to any third party or use it for its own use at variance with the purpose for which it has been provided.

405. The acquirer shall conceal the documents and messages received from the provider and not disclose them to any third parties unless it is clear from the contract or from the nature of the documents and messages that the provider does not intend to keep them secret. A third party is not deemed to be an employee or a person who takes part in the provider's business unless bound by the non-disclosure obligation by the provider.

406. If the contract has been made for an indefinite period, the notice of termination comes into effect upon the expiration of one year from the end of a calendar month in which the notice of termination was delivered to the other party.

§6. Scope of Exclusive Rights

407. The cultivator's right holder has the exclusive right to use a protected variety within the territory of the Czech Republic, which consists in a licence to treat the propagation material of the variety in the following manners:

(a) production or propagation;
(b) treatment for the propagation purposes;
(c) offering for sale;
(d) selling or other means of putting the material into circulation;

(e) placing the material on the market in Member States and exporting it into third countries;
(f) placing the material on the market in Member States and importing it from third countries;
(g) storing the material for the purposes listed above.

408. This also applies to the harvested material of a protected variety, including whole plants and parts of plants, provided that it has been obtained from the propagation material of the protected variety without the licence of the cultivator's right holder who could not exercise these rights to the aforesaid propagation material. The protection similarly applies to:

(a) the varieties that are essentially derived from a protected variety;
(b) the varieties that do not differ from a protected variety;
(c) the varieties whose production requires repeated use of a protected variety.

409. Varieties are considered to be essentially derived from another variety if:

(a) they are predominantly derived from the original variety or from a variety which is essentially derived from the original variety;
(b) they differ from the original variety; and
(c) except for differences resulting from the derivation, they substantially coincide with the original variety in the manifestation of elements resulting from the genotype or a combination of the genotype of the original variety.

410. The essentially derived varieties may be obtained in particular by the selection of a natural or induced mutation or somaclonal aberration, by the selection of a different individual from the plants of the original variety, by the reverse hybridization or by the transformation by means of genetic engineering methods. Where an essentially derived variety is a protected variety, the right of the cultivator's right holder to the original variety with respect to the essentially derived variety is restricted only to the right to provide the cultivator's right holder of this variety a licence to use it. The holder of the cultivator's rights to the essentially derived variety may handle the variety only with the licence of the holder of the cultivator's rights to the original variety.

§7. Limitations of the Scope of Protection: Compulsory Licences

411. The protective rights do not apply to the treatment of the protected variety material sold in the Czech Republic or otherwise put into circulation by the holder of the cultivator's rights or with his licence, nor to the treatment concerning each material derived therefrom unless it concerns:

(a) further propagation of the aforesaid varieties; or

(b) the export of the material of such varieties, which enables their further propagation, into a country that does not protect varieties of the plant genus or the strain to which the variety belongs; this does not apply if the material is intended for final consumption.

412. Where a protected variety has been granted the Community plant variety right, the protective rights cannot be exercised during the force thereof. The Ministry of Agriculture may grant a forced licence to use a protected variety to one or more persons upon their application if the holder of the cultivator's rights refuses to grant the licence, or licence within a required extent, to the use thereof, and if the use is in public interest. The Ministry announces the forced licence award to the Institute.

413. Upon granting the forced licence, the Ministry stipulates the terms and conditions, duration and scope of the exploitation, including the standard price of the licence belonging to the holder of the cultivator's rights. After one year following the forced licence award, each party to the forced licensing procedure may request in writing that the Ministry revokes or changes the decision to grant a forced licence. The grounds of the application may only be based on a change of the circumstances under which the decision has been issued.

414. The Ministry may grant a forced licence to an essentially derived variety upon the application of the holder of the cultivator's right to the variety concerned if the holder of the cultivator's rights to the original variety refuses to grant a licence to use the essentially derived variety and provided that the use thereof is in public interest.

415. If the owner of a patent to a biotechnological invention cannot make use of the patent without infringing an earlier right to a protected variety, such owner may apply for a forced licence to the non-exclusive use of the variety. The Ministry shall grant a forced licence if the patent owner unsuccessfully requested the consent of the cultivator's rights holder with the use of the protected variety and if the invention protected by the patent represents an important technical progress of considerable economic significance compared to the protected variety.

416. The reasons why a given invention represents an important technical advance of considerable economic significance compared to the protected variety may consist in particular in the improvement in cultivation practices, the environment, processes facilitating the use of genetic diversity, improvement of quality, yield, resistance, or the improvement in adaptation to specific climate conditions or environmental conditions. The amount of the corresponding licence fee is determined by the Ministry. In this case, the holder of the cultivator's rights has the right to a cross-licence (counter-licence) to use the biotechnological invention.

417. If the holder of the cultivator's rights has been granted a forced licence to use a biotechnological invention, the patent owner has the right to a cross-licence (counter-licence) to use a protected variety.

§8. DURATION OF PROTECTION

418. The protective rights to a protected variety last until the end of the 25th year following the year in which the protective rights have been lawfully granted. The protective rights to protected varieties of woody plants, hops, grapevine and potatoes last until the end of the 30th year following the year in which the protective rights have been lawfully granted.

419. Within the period between the submission of the application and the final granting of the protective rights to a variety, the holder of the cultivator's rights is entitled to a reasonable compensation from any person who treated the variety within that period in manners which, in that particular period, are subject to a licence of the holder of the cultivator's right.

420. The protective rights extinguish upon the expiration of the period stipulated by this Act, or in the case that the holder of the cultivator's rights fails to pay the maintenance fee in time despite the invitation sent by the Institute within a period stipulated by the Institute, or if the holder notifies the Institute in writing that it surrenders the protective rights.

421. The Institute revokes the protective rights prior to the expiration of their time in the event that the protected variety no longer meets the uniformity and stability conditions, or in the case that the holder of the cultivator's rights fails to meet the obligation to maintain the protected variety for the whole period of the right's duration or submitting specimen of the protected variety for inspection.

422. If it turns out subsequently that, at the time of the issuance of the cultivator's certificate upon which the protective rights have been lawfully granted, the conditions for granting the protective rights have actually not been met, the Institute revokes the cultivator's certificate; in this case, the protective rights are viewed as if they have never been granted.

§9. INFRINGEMENT AND REMEDIES

423. The cultivator or the processor commits an administrative infraction if:

(a) it fails to notify the holder of the cultivator's right in writing, on its request, of the name, or the names, surname, place of business and identification number or the trade name or title, registered office, identification number and legal form (if it is a legal entity);
(b) it fails to provide the holder of the cultivator's rights with the documents relating to its identification, and with the documents concerning the quantity of farming seed corn, or seedling/planting supplied to him for treatment, respectively, as well as with the resulting quantity of treated seed corn, or seedling/

planting, respectively, and with the documents regarding the date, place of treatment and identification details of a person for whom the treatment has been carried out.

424. The processor commits an administrative infraction if he fails to notify the holder of the cultivator's rights in writing, on its requests, of the information regarding the quantity of seed corn, or seedling/planting, respectively, supplied to him for treatment, as well as of the resulting quantity of the treated seed corn, or seedling/planting, respectively, and of the information about the date, place of treatment and identification details of a person for whom the treatment has been carried out.

425. The processor who carries out treatment of the propagation material of protected varieties commits an administrative infraction if he fails to report this activity to the Institute. The processor commits an administrative infraction if he fails to notify the holder of the cultivator's rights in writing, on its request, of the information:

(a) about the extent of the use of farming seed corn or seedling/planting, respectively, including the information about the scope of the use of certified propagation material of the variety concerned;
(b) about the processor who carried out the treatment for him in the case that he did not treat the seed corn, or the seedling/planting, respectively, by himself.

426. The holder of the cultivator's rights commits an infraction if he fails to provide the grower with the following information in writing:

(a) the amount of the payment the holder will charge for the use of the farming seed corn or, as the case may be, seedling/planting by sowing or planting;
(b) the standard price of a licence for a given variety in the respective calendar year.

427. A fine up to CZK 500,000 may be imposed for such infractions which are heard, and the fines are collected by the Institute. The following entities are entitled to enforce the rights protected by this Act:

(a) the holder of the cultivator's rights;
(b) the licensee with respect to a protected variety; or
(c) the professional organization authorized to represent holders of the cultivator's rights.

428. The licensee may enforce the rights only with the consent granted by the holder of the cultivator's rights. The consent is not required if the holder of the cultivator's rights has not instigated proceedings concerning a breach of or a threat to the right within one month following the delivery of the licensee's notification of the breach of or the threat to the right.

429. The holder of the cultivator's rights, the licensee with respect to a protected variety or the professional organization authorized to represent holders of the cultivator's rights may request information about the origin and distribution channels of the propagation material or harvested material of a variety or the services violating the law from a person who infringed the rights protected by this Act or from a person who, for the purpose of direct or indirect economic or commercial benefit:

(a) held the propagation material or harvested material of a variety violating the law;
(b) used services violating the law;
(c) provided services utilized for the activities violating the law; or
(d) has been defined by the person mentioned under (a), (b) or (c) as the person participating in the production, processing, storing or distribution of the propagation material or harvested material of a variety or in the provision of services.

430. The disputes arising from legal relationships established by the Act to Protect Varieties of Plants are heard and decided by courts. In the case of an unauthorized interference with a right protected by this Act, the entitled person whose right has been endangered or breached may demand that the breaching party refrains from such act and removes the defective state. If the interference caused damage, the aggrieved party has the right to compensation. In the case of non-pecuniary damage, the aggrieved party has the right to a reasonable satisfaction which may also consist of a pecuniary performance.

431. A competent court may decide upon the proposal of an entitled person that the propagation material or harvested material of a variety, which was treated at variance with the exclusive right of the holder of the cultivator's rights, is withdrawn from the market or destroyed, unless the violation of the right could be removed otherwise and the destruction thereof would be disproportionate to the breach in question. Where remedies are directed to the propagation material or harvested material of a variety, which is not owned by the person infringing the exclusive right of the holder of the cultivator's rights, the court shall consider third-party rights, in particular the rights of consumers and persons acting in good faith.

432. The entitled person may also lodge claims at the court against the brokers whose means or services are used by third parties for the infringement of rights. In its decision, the court may grant the entitled person, whose motion has been satisfied, the right to publish the judgment at the costs of the infringing party who has not succeeded in the dispute, and, given the circumstances, to determine the scope, form and manner of the publication thereof.

§10. Overlapping and Relation to Other Intellectual Property Laws

433. Similarly to the author's work or invention, a new plant variety is a unique intellectual creation – invention – of its 'author', i.e., the cultivator in this particular case. However, a plant variety cannot be considered an invention or author's work as it is subject to a special protection.

Chapter 8. Chip Protection

§1. Sources: Legislation

434. The protection of chips is regulated by Act no. 529/1991 Coll. providing for the protection of topography of semiconductor products, as amended.

§2. Subject Matter of the Protection

435. The subject matter of the protection is the topography of semiconductor products resulting from the creative activity of their originator, which are not common in the semiconductor industry. The protection hereunder also applies to the parts of topography that are usable separately as well as to the depictions serving to produce topography.

436. If a topography is made up of elements that are generally known, it is protected only if the combination of the elements meets the conditions stated above. The protection does not apply to the technology used for the creation of a topography or a semiconductor product, nor to the information stored within the product.

437. The topography is understood as a series of fixed or coded mutually related depictions illustrating a three-dimensional permanent arrangement of the layers of which the semiconductor product is composed, while each depiction represents a pattern of one layer of the semiconductor product, or a part thereof, or the surface of the semiconductor product in the individual stages of production, or parts thereof.

438. The semiconductor product means a final or an interim form of a microelectronic product intended to fulfil electronic functions, which is composed of a base body containing a layer of semiconductor material and at least one layer of conductive, insulating or semiconducting material in a predetermined configuration.

§3. Conditions of Protection

439. The right to protect topography belongs to its originator or its legal successor. If a topography has been created in order to fulfil a task related to employment or a similar relationship, the right to protection belongs to the employer or to the person for whom it has been created under a contract, unless the contract stipulates otherwise.

440. Based on an application which may be filed by anyone, the Office shall expunge topography from the register in the following cases:

(a) if the topography subject to the protection is not registered;

(b) if the application for a topography has not been filed within two years following the first, but not hidden, business utilization of the topography, or if the right to protection has extinguished;
(c) if the applicant or owner of the topography is a person who could not exercise the right to protection because he/she was not a Czech citizen or a person whose residence or business address is in a state which is a member of the World Trade Organization or if the state in which the applicant has his/her residence or seat is not a member of the World Trade Organization and does not grant protection under the condition of reciprocity;
(d) if the submitted documents do not comply with the semiconductor product attached to the application.

441. The expungement of a topography from the register has the same effect as if the topography has never been registered. An application for the expungement of a topography must be substantiated and, at the same time, the applicant must produce the evidence upon which the application is based. The Office invites the owner of the topography to make a statement to the application for the expungement thereof from the register within a specified time.

442. Based on a proposal, the Office shall take away the protection from the owner of a registered topography if it ascertains from a court decision that the owner has no right to the protection of the topography as it actually has not been the originator thereof. The proposal for the withdrawal of the protection may be filed only by the person who, according to the court's decision, has the right to protection of the topography, or his legal successor.

443. On request of the person eligible for the protection of the topography, which must be filed within one month following the final and conclusive court decision, the Office shall register this person as the topography owner. If a request for the deregistration is not filed, the Office shall deregister the topography by virtue of office.

§4. Formalities (Procedure for Granting and Obtaining Protection)

444. Anyone who wishes to exercise the right to protection of topography must file a written application for the topography registration with the Office. A separate application must be filed for each individual topography.

445. The application must contain:

(a) a request for the registration of topographies stating the title of the topography concerned;
(b) the documents enabling the identification of the topography and, optionally, the semiconductor itself containing the topography;
(c) the date of the first, but not hidden, business use of the topography if it is earlier than the application date;

(d) a certificate documenting the acquisition of the right to protection of the topography and the data demonstrating the right to protection of the topography.

446. The applicant is entitled to define some of the requested documents allowing the identification of the topography, or the parts thereof, as trade or production secrets. In this case, the documents must be submitted in another version where the respective parts defined as trade or production secrets are illegible; however, the documents cannot be defined as a trade or production secret as a whole.

447. If the application meets the conditions stipulated by law, the Office shall enter the topography into the register. The Office shall issue a certificate of the topography registration to the applicant whose topography has been entered into the register and announce the registration of the topography in the Bulletin of the Industrial Property Office.

448. If the application fails to comply with the requirements stipulated by law, the Office shall invite the applicant to remove the shortcomings within a specified time. Should the applicant fail to remove the shortcomings in question within the specified time, the Office would discontinue the application procedure. The applicant must be notified of this consequence upon the specification of the time limit. If the application has been filed by an ineligible person or after the expiration of a two year time following the first, but not hidden, business use of the topography, the Office shall dismiss the application.

§5. Ownership and Transfer (Assignment – Licenses)

449. The right to protect a topography belongs to its originator or its legal successor. If a topography has been created in order to fulfil a task related to employment or a similar relationship, the right to protection belongs to the employer or the person for whom it has been created upon a contract, unless the contract stipulates otherwise.

450. The right may be assigned only upon a licence agreement. By the licence agreement, the provider grants the acquirer a licence to exercise the right to protect a topography within an agreed limited or unlimited scope and the acquirer undertakes to pay the provider a fee, unless the parties have agreed otherwise.

451. The licence comes into effect against third parties by the registration in the list of rights to protect topography managed by the Industrial Property Office. The acquirer is not obliged to make use of the licence unless the right's duration depends on the execution thereof.

452. In the event of an exclusive licence, the provider has no right to grant the same licence to a third party for as long as the exclusive licence is in force. Unless expressly agreed otherwise, the provider shall also refrain from exercising the right to which he has granted the exclusive licence.

453. If, during the force of the exclusive licence provided to the acquirer, the provider grants the licence to a third party without the acquirer's written consent, the licence will not be created. However, if a non-exclusive licence was granted prior to the provision of the exclusive licence, it will remain in force. If a non-exclusive licence has been granted, the provider is entitled to exercise the right to which he has granted the non-exclusive licence and grant it to a third party.

454. The licensee may grant a licence component fully or in part to a third party only if it has been agreed upon in the licence agreement. The licensee may assign the licence to a third party fully or in part only with the consent of the licence provider. The consent must be granted in the written form. Where a business establishment or a part thereof, which forms an independent unit of a business establishment, has been transferred, the consent of the provider with the licence assignment is requested only if it has been specifically agreed upon.

455. If a fee or the method of the determination thereof has not been agreed, the contract is nevertheless valid, provided that:

(a) the parties' negotiation regarding the conclusion of the contract implies their intention to execute a contract for value without determining the fee; in such a case, the acquirer shall pay the provider a standard fee which is customary at the time of the contract execution under similar contractual conditions and for such law; or
(b) the parties to the contract agree that the licence is granted free of charge.

456. If the fee has been agreed as depending on the proceeds from the use of the licence, the acquirer shall enable the provider to check the respective accounting entries or other documentation in order to ascertain the actual amount of the fee. Where the acquirer provides the information to the provider which is defined by the acquirer as confidential, the provider must not disclose it to any third party or use it for its own use at variance with the purpose for which it has been provided.

457. The acquirer shall conceal the documents and messages received from the provider and not disclose them to any third parties unless it is clear from the contract or from the nature of the documents and messages that the provider does not intend to keep them secret. A third party is not deemed to be an employee or a person who takes part in the provider's business unless bound by the non-disclosure obligation by the provider.

458. If the contract has been made for an indefinite period, the notice of termination comes into effect upon the expiration of one year from the end of a calendar month in which the notice of termination was delivered to the other party.

§6. Scope of Exclusive Rights

459. Without the consent (the licence) of the owner of a topography, no one may:

(a) reproduce a topography or its separately usable parts, and make a representation of the topography for production purposes;
(b) produce a semiconductor product which contains a protected topography;
(c) use a topography or a semiconductor for commercial purposes which contains a protected topography or its separately usable parts, as well as a representation of the topography that serves for the production thereof or import them for that purpose.

460. The effects of protection may be exercised against third parties after the registration of a topography in the register. If the owner of a topography proves that a third party has fraudulently reproduced the topography prior to the registration date, or used it for commercial purposes, or imported it for these purposes, the owner has the right to seek a reasonable compensation from the third party.

§7. Limitations of the Scope of Protection

461. The effects of topography protection do not apply to:

(a) activities carried out for non-commercial purposes;
(b) reproductions of a topography for the purpose of analysis, research, development or education;
(c) commercial use of a topography created on the basis of an analysis, research or development, provided that this other topography is a result of creative activity of the originator thereof and is not common in the semiconductor products' industry;
(d) consecutive commercial use of a topography or a semiconductor product containing a protected topography put into circulation by the owner of the topography or with its explicit consent.

462. The effects of topography protection do not apply to a person who obtains in good faith a semiconductor product containing a protected topography which was put into circulation without the consent of the owner of the topography. From the time that this person learnt, or it could be reasonably assumed that he could have learnt, that the product contains a protected topography, such person is obliged to pay the topography owner on his request a reasonable compensation for further commercial use of the product; the amount of the fee depends on the scope of further commercial use.

§8. Duration of Protection

463. The right to protect topography extinguishes fifteenth years after the creation thereof, provided that the topography has not been used in commerce otherwise but covertly or it has not been registered with the Industrial Property Office.

464. The protection of topography is established:

(a) on the first, but not hidden, commercial use of topography, provided that the topography was the subject matter of a due application filed with the Office within two years following the use thereof; or
(b) on the application date, provided that the topography has not been used in commerce before, or it has been used only covertly.

The duration of the topography protection terminates ten years following the end of the calendar year in which the protection was established.

§9. Infringement and Remedies

465. A person commits an infraction by using a protected topography without authorization. For this infraction, a fine up to CZK 250,000 of a ban on activity may be imposed. If the infraction is committed by a legal entity or a natural entity – an entrepreneur – the publication of the decision on the infraction may be also imposed. The infraction is heard by the municipal council of a municipality with extended jurisdiction and cannot be dealt with by order imposed in situ.

§10. Overlapping and Relation to Other Intellectual Property Laws

466. Similarly to author's work or invention, new chips represent a unique intellectual creation – the invention of the 'author', i.e., the cultivator, in this case. However, a chip cannot be an invention nor an author's work as it is subject to special protection.

Chapter 9. Trade Secrets/Confidential Information

§1. Sources: Legislation

467. The regulation of trade secret is contained in section 504 of the Civil Code.

§2. The Protection of Trade Secrets/Confidential Information

468. The trade secret is an intangible asset and it is thus subject to the protection provided to the ownership right. At the same time, it is also protected by means of unfair competition law. The special facts of unfair competition also include a breach of trade secret. This means an act by which the acting person communicates to another person, makes available or uses for himself or for another person a trade secret which may be used in competition and of which the acting person learnt:

(a) by being entrusted with the trade secret or the trade secret was otherwise made available to him based on his employment with the competitor or based on other relationship to the competitor, or in the course of discharge of his office to which he was summoned by court or by other authority; or
(b) by his own or someone else's act at variance with the law.

469. The facts of the delict are also fulfilled if the acting person uses trade secret directly for himself or for another person. The use of trade secret is understood as the application of the information (procedures, instructions, etc.) arising from trade secret, e.g., for production.

470. As per the facts of the case, there is an exception represented by the fact that it is not a competitor's act but the acts that are in a certain relation to the competitor. It does not involve just any breach of the right to trade secret but solely a breach of the right to trade secret which may be used in competition.

471. An unauthorized disclosure means the provision of information which is not in compliance with the law or with the regulations passed on the basis of the law. Therefore, the unauthorized disclosure of trade secret does not occur if an employee is instructed to disclose the information in question, or the information ceases to be subject to trade secret, e.g., because it becomes a public domain, or the competitor no longer intends to conceal it.

472. Making trade secret accessible means that the information subject to trade secret is still not disclosed but someone is allowed to obtain the information. The use of trade secret then means a direct application of the information which forms the trade secret. Trade secrets may be accessed either legally, based on a certain relationship to the competitor, or illegally. In the latter case we are speaking of the so-called espionage.

473. The persons whose rights have been infringed or endangered by unfair competition may request that the infringer refrains from such acting (by dilatory action or action to repel claim) and remove the defective state (by removal action). They can also request a reasonable satisfaction which may be also granted in cash, damages and release of unjust enrichment.

474. The legal remedies against unfair competition are thus exclusively private and the state does not intervene in the protection of the rights violated by unfair competition. The protection of these rights is exclusively a matter of the competitors or customers or persons who defend their interests. The purity of competition is thus guarded and protected by the participants themselves, while the state does not intervene and only creates prerequisites for the protection of rights of individual entities in the context of their private protection.

475. It is not necessary for the creation of the right to a reasonable compensation that the person who perpetrates an act of unfair competition would do so intentionally. A reasonable satisfaction may be either moral (e.g., an apology published in daily press) or financial. The amount of a reasonable financial satisfaction is not bound to the occurrence of damage and is subject to a court decision on request of the aggrieved party; the amount cannot be established on the basis of evidence documenting the damage but only by the proof of the intensity of the non-material harm incurred by the aggrieved party.

476. Reasonable financial satisfaction is also not bound to the amount of damage incurred and the title to damages cannot be replaced by claiming it. Therefore, it does not serve as a flat-rate compensation for damage and it is not possible to circumvent the necessity to prove the amount of the damage incurred. In addition to a brief regulation by the Civil Code, the means of legal protection against unfair competition also include the actions regulated only by the Civil Proceedings Code, such as the preliminary injunction, declaratory action, etc.

477. The judicial remedies for the protection against unfair competition are the following:

(a) dilatory action (i.e., the action to repel a claim);
(b) removal action;
(c) action to grant a reasonable satisfaction, which may be:
   – moral;
   – financial;
(d) action for damages or lost profit;
(e) action to release unjust enrichment;
(f) declaratory action to declare that a competitor has committed an act of unfair competition;
(g) preliminary injunction;
(h) action for obtaining evidence.

478. It follows from the foregoing that it is also possible to file an action to declare the obligation to refrain from a certain act of unfair competition in the future. The declaration of this obligation cannot be requested if the competitor no longer perpetrates the defective act and the repetition thereof is not impending in the future. On the other hand, the right to claim removal of a defective state is directed to removal of the effects of unfair competition which have already occurred and continue to exist. The removal of a defective state may consist, e.g., in the withdrawal of defective products, withdrawal of mitigating statements or change of a trade name.

479. This claim, however, is not identical to the claim for damages or release of unfair enrichment, which, in addition to the claim for removal of a defective state, may exist separately. A legal person entitled to defend the rights of competitors or customers may also enforce the right to have the infringer refrain from wrongful acting and remove the defective state, except for the cases of sponging on one's reputation, bribing, mitigating and violating trade secret. These persons are not competitors or customers; these can be, e.g., the associations of entrepreneurs in a certain industry or consumer associations.

480. If a consumer seeks to have a person committing an act of unfair competition refrain or remove the defective state in the cases of a breach of general clause, misleading advertising, misleading designation of goods or services, unpermitted comparative advertising, likelihood of confusion and the threat to health or environment, the suspect infringer must prove that he has not committed the act of unfair competition. Therefore, transferring the burden of proof to the defendant is valid only if a consumer, not just any customer, claims the right.

481. The burden of proof on the part of the defendant also applies to actions for damages as to the question whether the damage was caused by unfair competition, and to their right to a reasonable satisfaction and release of unjust enrichment, but only in the case that the right is claimed by the consumer and not by just any customer. However, the petitioner, i.e., the person who has been affected or aggrieved by unfair competition, even though it is a consumer, must always prove the amount of damages incurred, the severity and scope of other harm, and the nature and scope of unjust enrichment.

Chapter 10. Geographical Indications and Appellations of Origin

482. The protection of appellations of origin and geographical indications is regulated by Act no. 452/2001 Coll., as amended. The appellation of origin is the name of a region, a certain place or a country used for the designation of goods produced in the territory, provided that the quality or properties of the goods are exclusively or predominantly caused by a specific geographical environment with its typical natural and human factors and the production, processing and preparation of such goods is carried out within a defined territory; the appellation of origin for agricultural products or foodstuff is also deemed to be the traditional geographical or non-geographical designations of goods produced within the defined territory, provided that the goods meet other conditions stipulated hereunder.

483. A geographical indication is the name of a territory used for the designation of the goods originating in that territory, provided that the goods have a certain quality, reputation or other properties which may be attributed to the geographical origin and provided that the production or processing or preparation of such goods is carried out within the defined territory.

484. The appellation of origin and geographical indication are registered in the register of appellations of origin and geographical indications managed by the Industrial Property Office.

485. An appellation of origin or a geographical indication, the exact wording of which may truly refer to a territory in which the goods are produced but it is still likely to make an impression that the goods come from another territory, cannot be registered as such.

486. If an applicant for registration of an appellation of origin or a geographical indication into a wine register ensures such a manner of use of the indications which is not capable of making an erroneous assumption about the actual origin of the goods, two or more appellations of origin or geographical indications may be registered which contain the same or similar (homonymous) wording of names of the territories while observing the principle of equal position of producers on the market.

487. A general designation of the kind of goods, irrespective of whether the goods come from a territory so defined, cannot be registered as an appellation of origin or a geographical indication. An appellation identical to an already protected appellation of origin, geographical indication, generally known trademark or registered trademark or an appellation identical to a name of a plant variety or animal breed which could, as a result of the compliance, lead to false assumptions regarding the actual origin of the goods, cannot be registered as an appellation of origin or a geographical indication.

488. The registration of an appellation of origin in the register may be applied for by an association of producers or processors for the goods produced or processed or prepared within a territory concerned. An individual natural or legal entity may apply for registration of an appellation of origin in the register if, at the application date, it is the only one to produce, process or prepare the goods within the territory in question.

489. The Office shall examine whether or not the appellation of origin specified in the application meets the conditions for the entry in the register. Where the appellation of origin is excluded from registration, or the appellation does not meet the conditions of registration stipulated by this Act, the Office shall dismiss the application. If the application for registration of an appellation of origin in the register contains any and all essential elements and the application is not rejected, the Office shall enter the appellation into the register and announce the registration in the Bulletin issued by the Industrial Property Office. The Office then shall issue a certificate of registration to the applicant.

490. The protection of an appellation of origin is created on the date of registration thereof and the protection period is not limited in time. Anyone who produces, processes and prepares goods of a corresponding quality or properties within a defined territory is entitled to use, in particular to place it on the goods concerned, a registered appellation of origin. A registered appellation of origin cannot be subject to a licence and must not be provided as a security.

491. An applicant for the registration of an appellation of origin may apply with the Office for a change in the specification thereof, in particular with respect to the development of scientific and technical knowledge or due to a redefinition of the territory concerned.

492. The authority responsible for checking the specification hereunder is, within the scope of the competence thereof, the State Agriculture and Food Inspection, the State Veterinary Administration or the Central Institute for Supervising and Testing in Agriculture. The authority shall issue binding awards or reports or certificates necessary for the registration of appellations of origin in the register. Along with the application for a change of specification of an agricultural product or foodstuff, or the application to revoke the registration of an appellation of origin of an agricultural product or foodstuff, or the application for registration of an appellation of origin of an agricultural product or foodstuff, the applicant or the petitioner, respectively, is obliged to submit an award of the aforesaid authority.

493. The Office shall revoke the registration of an appellation of origin if it ascertains upon a proposal of an affected person or a respective authority or upon its own initiative if:

(a) the appellation of origin has already been registered but it does not meet the conditions stipulated by this Act; in this case, the appellation of origin is viewed as it has never been registered;

(b) the conditions stipulated for the registration of appellations of origin have ceased;
(c) the product for which the appellation of origin has been registered does not meet the requirements stipulated by the specification of an agricultural product or foodstuff according to the award of the respective authority, and the requirements have not been met even within an additional time specified by the authority.

494. Under a directly applicable EU regulation concerning a product with the origin in the Czech Republic, or in a cross-border geographical territory, the application for registration of an appellation of origin or a geographical indication, which is used in the Czech Republic in connection with the aforesaid product, is filed with the Office.

495. The Office shall request that the Ministry of Agriculture provides a statement to the application for a Community registration whether or not the designation under application contains a name which has become generic, a name of a plant variety or an animal breed or a homonymous name. For this purpose, the Office stipulates a time limit which must not be shorter than ten days. If the Ministry of Agriculture fails to provide its statement within the specified time limit, it is assumed that it has no comments or reservations to the application concerned.

496. If an application for the Community registration concerns a name defining a geographical territory which overlaps in the territory of another EU Member State, the natural or legal entities settled within the territory of that state or the natural entities residing in that state, respectively, have the same rights in the proceedings held before the Office as the natural or legal entities settled in the Czech Republic or the natural entities residing in the Czech Republic.

497. Opposition shall be filed in writing within three months following the publication of the application for the Community registration in the Bulletin. The opposition must contain the grounds thereof and produce the evidence that the designation under application fails to meet the conditions stipulated by the EU regulation directly applicable to the registration in the register managed by the European Commission. The Office shall inform the Ministry of Agriculture about the opposition filed therewith.

498. The registered designations are protected against:

(a) any direct or indirect commercial use of a registered designation for the goods not covered by the registration, provided that the goods are comparable with the goods registered under the designation, or where the use of the designation profits from good reputation of the protected designation;
(b) any misuse, imitation or reminiscence, even if the actual origin of goods is stated, or the protected designation is translated or accompanied by expressions such as 'kind', 'type', 'method', 'by way of', 'imitated' or by a similar expression;

(c) any other misleading or deceptive indication of a geographical origin, nature or essential characteristics of the goods on the inner or outer packaging, advertisement materials or documents relating to the respective goods, as well as against the use of transportation packaging that is likely to make a false impression regarding its origin;
(d) any other types of conduct which might lead to false assumptions as to the true origin of the goods.

499. A registered designation cannot become a generic designation of goods. Anyone may make a claim at a respective court that the use of a registered designation for comparable goods, which fails to meet the conditions for the use of an appellation of origin or a geographical indication, is prohibited and that the goods labelled in a manner that has endangered or infringed the rights associated with the registered appellation of origin or a geographical indication, respectively, is withdrawn from the market.

Selected Bibliography

Dobichovský, Tomáš. *Aktuální otázky práva autorského a práv prmyslových: europeizace českého práva duševního vlastnictví – harmonizační zmny v legislativ a výkladu*. Praha: *Univerzita Karlova v. Praze*, 2017. Právnická fakulta. ISBN 978-80-87975-75-6.

Jakl, Ladislav. *Duševní vlastnictví a jeho právní ochrana*. 2. vydání. Praha: Metropolitan University Prague Press, 2017. ISBN 978-80-87956-50-2.

Jakl, Ladislav. *Nový občanský zákoník a duševní vlastnictví*. Praha: Metropolitan University Prague Press, 2012. ISBN 978-80-86855-87-5.

Koukal, Pavel. *Právní ochrana designu – prmyslové vzory, autorská díla*. Praha: Wolters Kluwer ČR, 2012. Právní monografie. ISBN 978-80-7357-886-2.

Kíž, Jan. *Aktuální otázky práva autorského a práv prmyslových: nové trendy a problémy aplikační praxe se zvláštním pihlédnutím k právu EU a judikatue SDEU*. Praha: Univerzita Karlova v Praze, 2016. Právnická fakulta. ISBN 978-80-87975-58-9.

Kíž, Jan. *Aktuální otázky práva autorského a práv prmyslových: reflexe komunitární regulace a vybrané aplikační problémy*. Praha: Univerzita Karlova v Praze, 2015. Právnická fakulta. ISBN 978-80-87975-41-1.

Kíž, Jan. *Aktuální otázky práva autorského a práv prmyslových: nový občanský zákoník a vybrané problémy evropského práva duševního vlastnictví – dopady na českou legislativu a praxi*. Praha: Univerzita Karlova v Praze, 2014. Právnická fakulta. ISBN 978-80-87975-15-2.

Kíž, Jan. *Aktuální otázky práva autorského a práv prmyslových: impulsy k novelizaci pedpis v oblasti duševního vlastnictví a revizi aplikační praxe = [Current problems of copyright and industrial property]*. Praha: Univerzita Karlova v Praze, 2012. Právnická fakulta. ISBN 978-80-87146-70-5.

Matjičný, Tomáš. *Kolektivní správa autorských práv*. Plze: Vydavatelství a nakladatelství Aleš Čenk, 2014. Pro praxi. ISBN 978-80-7380-528-9.

Pospíšil, Michal. *Specifika ochrany duševních práv v České republice a ve svt: k poct prof. Ladislavu Jaklovi*. Praha: Metropolitan University Prague Press, 2018. ISBN 978-80-87956-79-3.

Smejkal, Vladimír. *Ochrana autorských práv u dl architektonických a urbanistických*. Praha: Informační centrum ČKAIT, 2013. ISBN 978-80-87438-47-3.

Srstka, Jií, Jan Barták & Tomáš Dobichovský et al. *Autorské právo a práva související: vysokoškolská učebnice*. Praha: Leges, 2017. Student. ISBN 978-80-7502-240-0.

Selected Bibliography

Šulc, Petr a Aleš BARTOŠ. *Autorské právo v otázkách a odpovdích.* Praha: Pierot, 2012. ISBN 978-80-7353-223-9.

Sýkorová, Pavla. *Autorské právo v architektue.* V. Praze: C.H. Beck, 2018. Právní praxe. ISBN 978-80-7400-705-7.

Valoušek, Martin. *Fotografie a právo: autorské právo a ochrana osobnosti ve vztahu k fotografii.* Praha: Leges, 2014. Praktik. ISBN 978-80-7502-043-7.

Index

The numbers here refer to paragraph numbers.

Index

Made in the USA
Monee, IL
18 October 2026

66041385R10072